EDITO

OSPREY
MILITARY

MEN-A

245

BRITISH L
UNITS 1914-18

Text by
RAY WESTLAKE
Colour plates by
MIKE CHAPPELL

Published in 1991 by
Osprey Publishing Ltd
59 Grosvenor Street, London W1X 9DA
© Copyright 1991 Osprey Publishing Ltd

ISBN 1 85532 168 8

Filmset in Great Britain
Printed through Bookbuilders Ltd, Hong Kong

For a catalogue of all books published by Osprey Military
please write to:

**The Marketing Manager,
Consumer Catalogue Department,
Osprey Publishing Ltd,
Michelin House, 81 Fulham Road,
London SW3 6RB**

THE BIRTH OF THE TERRITORIALS

In his Army Reforms of 1906/07 the Secretary of State for War, Richard Burdon Haldane, provided for an expeditionary force—the Regular Army supplemented by the old Militia (now called the Special Reserve); and a new organisation intended for home defence—the Territorial Force. The new 'Citizen's Army' was formed by the transfer of the Honourable Artillery Company, Imperial Yeomanry and Volunteer Force, all with many years of service and tradition.

Existing since 1537 and having been chartered by Henry VIII, the Honourable Artillery Company proudly claimed its seniority among not only the auxiliary forces but the Regulars too. Likewise many units of the Yeomanry could justifiably claim great age, a fair number having origins in those corps sanctioned in 1794 when invasion from France was a serious threat. Again, in 1859, a possible attack on home shores saw the formation of the Volunteer Force.

Created under the Territorial and Reserve Forces Act, 7 Ed. VII, cap. 9, dated 2 August 1907, the Territorial Force came into being on 1 April 1908. The 1907 Act provided for the setting up of County Territorial Force Associations whose responsibility it was to see to the administration of units in their charge at all times, except when called out for training or actual military service, or when embodied. These Associations also handled financial matters and recruiting, and were expected to hand over equipped and complete, when required for the General Officer Commanding-in-Chief to train and handle in the field, all units in its charge. There were at this time no units in Ireland, the Territorial Force being confined to England, Scotland and Wales.

In a Special Army Order dated 18 March 1908 (para. 1) the organisation of the Territorial Force was set out. It stated that the Territorial Force was to be modelled on the Regular Army and should consist of 14 Divisions, 14 Mounted Brigades, certain Army Troops and special troops for defended ports, the latter consisting of such artillery and engineers as could not be provided by divisions. This same Army Order also explained the main points in which the organisation of the Territorial Force deviated from that of the Regular Army. The Yeomanry were organised for the purpose of training and administration in regiments of four squadrons instead of three, as in the Regular cavalry. A whole regiment of Yeomanry was allocated as divisional cavalry, instead of two squadrons, as in a Regular division. Horse, Field and Mountain Artillery were to be on a four-gun instead of a six-gun battery basis.

Under the conditions of the new system the Territorial Force was, if embodied, liable to be called out for service in any part of the United Kingdom, but it could not be ordered to go overseas. There were, however, provisions for other forms of service if required—the Special and Imperial Service Sections. The Special Service Section comprised members of Territorial units who had volunteered to be called out in case of national emergency, whether a

The white metal Imperial Service badge or brooch, worn on the right breast by men of units which volunteered for overseas service. (Unless otherwise credited, all photographs are from the author's collection)

No. 4 Company, Hampshire Royal Garrison Artillery, Cliff End Camp, 1909. Note the white leather 1888 pattern equipment being worn with both full and service dress. No. 4 Company was from Portsmouth, and served throughout the war on coastal defences.

state of embodiment was in operation or not. These men were required to be passed fit for the duties given them and were expected to serve under special conditions for a period not exceeding one month.

Officers and men of the peacetime Territorial Force could also offer to serve outside the United Kingdom in time of national emergency. Under the conditions set out for the Imperial Service Section, a Territorial could undertake to serve abroad, but only with his own unit, or with part of his own unit: he could not be drafted as an individual to any other unit except at his own request. Upon 90 per cent of a unit's strength having volunteered for overseas service, the words 'Imperial Service' were placed in the Army List after its title.

ORGANISATION IN 1914

The several Arms of the Territorial Force were as those for the Regular Army, its cavalry being known as Yeomanry. There were infantry battalions (some consisting of cyclists and unique to the TF), artillery, engineers, supply and medical formations, together with a special unit set up for the training of officers. Leading civil and railway engineers provided an officers-only corps, while trained nurses formed the Territorial Force Nursing Staff. There were also officers of the Army Veterinary Corps and Chaplains serving with Territorial Force units.

The following tables give a complete listing of all Territorial Force units that existed at the outbreak of war in 1914. The headquarters of each appears in brackets alongside its title.

Yeomanry Regiments

There were originally, in 1908, 56 regiments of Yeomanry each comprising four squadrons, and forming part of, or attached to, one or other of the new mounted brigades. In 1913 King Edward's Horse (The King's Overseas Dominions Regiment) was transferred to the Special Reserve, its place being taken in the following year by the formation of the Welsh Horse just after war was declared. Also in 1914 the Scottish Horse, then with two regiments, formed a third. Yeomanry regiments in 1914 were as follows:

Ayrshire (Ayr)	Royal North Devon
Bedfordshire (Bedford)	(Barnstaple)
Berkshire (Reading)	Dorset (Sherborne)
Buckinghamshire	Essex (Colchester)
(Buckingham)	Fife and Forfar
Cheshire (Chester)	(Kirkcaldy)
Denbighshire (Wrexham)	Glamorgan (Bridgend)
Derbyshire (Derby)	Gloucestershire
Royal 1st Devon (Exeter)	(Gloucester)

Hampshire (Winchester)
Hertfordshire (Hertford)
Royal East Kent
(Canterbury)
West Kent (Maidstone)
Lanarkshire (Lanark)
Lanarkshire, Royal
Glasgow (Yorkhill)
Lancashire Hussars
(Liverpool)
Duke of Lancaster's Own
(Manchester)
Leicestershire
(Leicester)
Lincolnshire (Lincoln)
City of London
(Finsbury Sq.)
1st County of London
(Chelsea)
2nd County of London
(Westminster)
3rd County of London
(St. John's Wood)
Lothians and Border
Horse (Edinburgh)

1st Lovat's Scouts
(Beauly)
2nd Lovat's Scouts
(Beauly)
Montgomeryshire
(Welshpool)
Norfolk (Norwich)
Northamptonshire
(Northampton)
Northumberland
(Newcastle-upon-Tyne)
Nottingham, Sherwood
Rangers (Retford)
Nottingham, South Notts
Hussars (Nottingham)
Oxfordshire (Oxford)
Pembrokeshire (Tenby)
1st Scottish Horse
(Dunkeld)
2nd Scottish Horse
(Aberdeen)
3rd Scottish Horse
Shropshire (Shrewsbury)
North Somerset (Bath)
West Somerset (Taunton)

Staffordshire (Stafford)
Suffolk (Bury St.
Edmunds)
Surrey (Clapham Park)
Sussex (Brighton)
Warwickshire (Warwick)
Welsh Horse (Cardiff)
Westmorland and
Cumberland (Penrith)

Royal Wiltshire
(Chippenham)
Worcestershire
(Worcester)
Yorkshire Dragoons
(Doncaster)
Yorkshire Hussars (York)
East Riding of Yorkshire
(Beverley)

Royal Horse Artillery

In 1908 eleven new units of horse artillery were formed, which together with the artillery section of the Honourable Artillery Company provided one battery and an ammunition column each for 13 of the 14 new mounted brigades. Mounted artillery for the remaining brigade was originally to come from Wiltshire, but recruiting did not go well and it fell to

Drivers and Trumpeters from one of the London Brigades, Royal Field Artillery, at camp in Kent in 1910. These men are wearing the old 60-round leather bandolier, obsolete since 1903. Note also the leather and steel leg-protectors worn by drivers on the right leg when mounted.

Warwickshire Yeomanry other ranks' full dress: dark blue with white facings and piping, 1911.

Hampshire in 1909 to provide the necessary personnel. Royal Horse Artillery formations were:

Ayrshire (Ayr)	Nottinghamshire
Berkshire (Reading)	(Nottingham)
Essex (Chelmsford)	West Riding (Rotherham)
Glamorgan (Port Talbot)	Shropshire (Shrewsbury)
Hampshire (Southampton)	Somerset (Taunton)
Inverness-shire	Warwickshire
(Inverness)	(Leamington)
Leicestershire (Leicester)	A Battery HAC (Finsbury)
	B Battery HAC (Finsbury)

Royal Field Artillery

Field artillery was provided for each of the 14 Territorial Force divisions—except the Highland Division—being made up of three field and one howitzer brigade; the Highland Division had two field and one howitzer, with a 4th Mountain Brigade that came under the Royal Garrison Artillery. Field brigades were made up of three batteries each, while the howitzer units comprised two. Each brigade had its own ammunition column, and was known—except for the 3rd Welsh, which was redesignated as Cheshire Brigade in 1913—by the name of its division, e.g. 1st East Anglian Brigade. Within the brigade, however, batteries were named, e.g. 1st Norfolk Battery, 2nd Norfolk Battery etc. Brigades in 1914 were as follows:

1st East Anglian (Norwich)	4th East Anglian
2nd East Anglian	(Hertford)
(Stratford)	1st Highland (Aberdeen)
3rd East Anglian	2nd Highland (Dundee)
(Howitzer) (Ipswich)	

3rd Highland (Howitzer)	1st North Midland
(Greenock)	(Grimsby)
1st Home Counties	2nd North Midland
(Brighton)	(Shelton)
2nd Home Counties	3rd North Midland
(Eastbourne)	(Wolverhampton)
3rd Home Counties	4th North Midland
(Dover)	(Howitzer) (Derby)
4th Home Counties	1st South Midland
(Howitzer) (Erith)	(Bristol)
1st East Lancashire	2nd South Midland
(Blackburn)	(Worcester)
2nd East Lancashire	3rd South Midland
(Manchester)	(Birmingham)
3rd East Lancashire	4th South Midland
(Bolton)	(Howitzer) (Coventry)
4th East Lancashire	1st Northumbrian
(Howitzer)	(Newcastle-upon-Tyne)
(Workington)	2nd Northumbrian (Hull)
1st West Lancashire	3rd Northumbrian
Liverpool)	(Seaham Harbour)
2nd West Lancashire	4th Northumbrian
(Preston)	(Howitzer)
3rd West Lancashire	(South Shields)
(Liverpool)	1st West Riding (Leeds)
4th West Lancashire	2nd West Riding
(Howitzer) (Liverpool)	(Bradford)
1st London (Bloomsbury)	3rd West Riding
2nd London (Woolwich)	(Sheffield)
3rd London (Finsbury)	4th West Riding
4th London (Howitzer)	(Howitzer) (Otley)
(Lewisham)	1st Welsh (Howitzer)
5th London (Lambeth)	(Swansea)
6th London (Brixton)	2nd Welsh (Cardiff)
7th London (Fulham)	Cheshire (Chester)
8th London (Howitzer)	4th Welsh (Newport)
(Woolwich)	1st Wessex
1st Lowland (Edinburgh)	(Portsmouth)
2nd Lowland (Irvine)	2nd Wessex (Howitzer)
3rd Lowland (Glasgow)	(Ryde)
4th Lowland (Howitzer)	3rd Wessex (Swindon)
(Glasgow)	4th Wessex (Exeter)

Royal Garrison Artillery

As previously mentioned the Highland Division included three field artillery brigades instead of four. Due to the mountainous character of the area in which its 4th Brigade was recruited—Argyllshire, Buteshire, Ross and Cromarty—its role was that of mountain artillery, and consequently the 4th Highland (Mountain) Brigade was placed into the Royal Garrison Artillery.

The next section of the Royal Garrison Artillery appeared in the Army List under the heading of 'Heavy'. This comprised 14 heavy batteries, one per division, each with its own ammunition column. Divisional Heavy Batteries were known by the name of their division but also included in their titles a geographical location. Units in 1914 were:

East Anglian (Essex)
(Stratford Green)
Highland (Fifeshire)
(Dunfermline)
Home Counties (Kent)
(Faversham)
1st Lancashire
(Liverpool)
2nd Lancashire
(Liverpool)
1st London (Islington)
2nd London (Islington)
Lowland (City of
Edinburgh)
North Midland
(Staffordshire)
(Stoke-on-Trent)
South Midland
(Warwickshire)
(Birmingham)
Northumbrian
(North Riding)
(Middlesbrough)
West Riding (York)
Welsh (Carnarvonshire)
(Bangor)
Wessex (Hampshire)
Cosham

Units formed under the heading of Royal Garrison Artillery (for defended ports) were located around naval bases and defended ports, and were required to man coast defences in case of general mobilisation.

Containing between two and ten garrison companies, and in some cases heavy batteries, each unit trained on the guns and works which it was to man in war. There were originally 16 units in this arm, but in 1910 the Sussex and Kent Royal Garrison Artillery, till then comprising three Sussex companies and seven Kent, was divided. Royal Garrison Artillery (for defended ports) units were:

Clyde (Port Glasgow)
Cornwall (Falmouth)
Devonshire (Plymouth)
Dorsetshire (Weymouth)
Durham (West Hartlepool)
East Riding (Hull)
Essex and Suffolk
(Dovercourt)
Forth (Edinburgh)
Glamorgan (Cardiff)
Hampshire (Southampton)
Kent (Sheerness)
Lancashire and Cheshire
(Liverpool)
Orkney (Kirkwall)
Pembroke (Milford Haven)
North Scottish (Broughty
Ferry)
Sussex (Brighton)
Tynemouth
(North Shields)

Royal Engineers

Prior to 1913 each of the 14 divisional engineer formations comprised two field and one telegraph company; but signal personnel were subsequently removed and organised as part of the Royal Engineers Signal Service. At a divisional level the same fourteen companies were retained but each was divided into four sections, one serving Headquarters and one each bearing the name of the infantry brigade that it served. Headquarters of Divisional Engineers and Signals were:

No. 1 Heavy Battery, Hampshire Royal Garrison Artillery at Lydd, 1911. This Southampton unit is seen practising with one of its 4.7 in. Quick Firing guns.

East Anglian (Bedford)
Highland (Aberdeen)
Home Counties
    (Eastbourne),
    Signals (Brighton)
East Lancashire
    (Old Trafford)
West Lancashire
    (St. Helens)
1st London
    (Bethnal Green)

2nd London (Chelsea)
Lowland (Rutherglen)
North Midland (Cannock),
    Signals (Hanley)
South Midland (Bristol)
Northumbrian
    (Newcastle-upon-Tyne)
West Riding (Sheffield)
Welsh (Cardiff)
Wessex (Bath),
    Signals (Exeter)

There were also Signal Companies (Army Troops), organised as three companies—one each Airline, Cable, Wireless—to each Command, viz. Northern (Leeds), Scottish (Glasgow), Southern (Birmingham), Western (Liverpool) and the London District (Westminster). It was the role of an airline company to set up non-permanent communications by laying temporary lines above the ground, using trees, bushes etc. Cable companies had the responsibility of more permanent telephone lines, usually buried; while wireless signallers worked their equipment from carts and wagons.

Included in the Coastal Defences system in 1914 were 18 Fortress Engineer formations. These varied in size from the City of Aberdeen unit, which comprised just one works company, to the Hampshire Fortress Engineers at Portsmouth with its three works and three electric lights companies:

City of Aberdeen	Hampshire (Portsmouth)
Cinque Ports (Dover)	Kent (Gillingham)
Cornwall (Falmouth)	Lancashire (Liverpool)
Devonshire (Plymouth)	Renfrewshire (Greenock)
Dorsetshire (Weymouth)	East Riding (Hull)
City of Dundee	North Riding
Durham (Jarrow)	(Middlesbrough)
City of Edinburgh	Sussex (Seaford)
Essex (Chelmsford)	Wiltshire (Swindon)
Glamorgan (Cardiff)	

Electrical Engineers had existed in the auxiliary forces since the formation of four companies in London during 1897. For the Territorial Force two units appeared under this heading—London, and Tyne (Headquarters North Shields)—their duties being to operate searchlights on coastal defences.

There also existed the Engineer and Railway Staff Corps. In existence since 1865, this all-officer organisation had its headquarters in London and acted as an advisory body regarding civil engineering and the operation of railways.

Two other units that were unique and formed part of the Royal Engineers Territorial Force were the London Balloon Company; and, from Crewe, the Cheshire Railway Battalion. Both of these were short-lived, the balloonists being disbanded in March 1913 while the railwaymen were removed from the Army List in 1912.

The Infantry

In the main infantry battalions were made up of eight companies each and numbered within their county regiments after the Regular and Special Reserve: e.g.

Private, City of London Yeomanry (Rough Riders), in French grey full dress with purple facings, c1911.

Note the distinctive collar badge comprising the letters 'RR' upon a spur.

Scottish Horse at camp, c1912. The two Yeomen standing left and right are wearing the Atholl grey full dress uniform introduced in 1908. The man seated at the right is wearing his Imperial Service brooch on the wrong side.

The Leicestershire Regiment, 1st and 2nd Battalions (Regular), 3rd Battalion (Special Reserve), 4th and 5th Battalions (Territorial). Only two battalions—the Brecknockshire Battalion of the South Wales Borderers, and the Buckinghamshire Battalion, Oxfordshire and Buckinghamshire Light Infantry—were known by name only. There also existed two units of less than battalion strength—the Ardeer Company, Royal Scots Fusiliers; and the two Shetland Companies of the Gordon Highlanders.

The Royal Fusiliers, King's Royal Rifle Corps and Rifle Brigade had no Territorial battalions, although the 1st, 2nd, 3rd, 4th Battalions of the London Regiment were affiliated to the former. There were no Territorial battalions in Irish Regiments, or the several regiments of Foot Guards. Territorial battalions forming part of Line regiments in 1914 were:

R. Scots: 4th, 5th, 6th (Edinburgh), 7th (Leith), 8th (Haddington), 9th (Edinburgh), 10th (Linlithgow)

R. W. Surrey: 4th (Croydon), 5th (Guildford)

E. Kent: 4th (Canterbury), 5th (Ashford)

King's Own: 4th (Ulverston), 5th (Lancaster)

N'd. Fus: 4th (Hexham), 5th, 6th (Newcastle), 7th (Alnwick)

R. Warwick: 5th, 6th (Birmingham), 7th (Coventry), 8th (Birmingham)

Liverpool: 5th, 6th (Liverpool), 7th (Bootle), 8th, 9th, 10th (Liverpool)

Norfolk: 4th (Norwich), 5th (East Dereham), 6th (Norwich)

Lincoln: 4th (Lincoln), 5th (Grimsby)

Devon: 4th (Exeter), 5th (Plymouth), 6th (Barnstaple), 7th (Exeter)

Suffolk: 4th (Ipswich), 5th (Bury St. Edmunds), 6th (Ipswich)

Somerset: 4th (Bath), 5th (Taunton)

W. Yorks: 5th (York), 6th (Bradford), 7th, 8th (Leeds)

E. Yorks: 4th, 5th (Hull)

Bedford: 5th (Bedford)

Leicester: 4th (Leicester), 5th (Loughborough)

Yorks: 4th (Northallerton), 5th (Scarborough)

Lancs. Fus: 5th (Bury), 6th (Rochdale), 7th, 8th (Salford)

RSF: 4th (Kilmarnock), 5th (Ayr), Ardeer Co.

Cheshire: 4th (Birkenhead), 5th (Chester), 6th (Stockport), 7th (Macclesfield)

Two Gloucestershire Territorials, from the Royal Gloucestershire Hussars (left) and 1st South Midland Brigade, Royal Field Artillery (right). Note the Yeoman's regimental cap badge—the Arms of the Duke of Beaufort.

Welsh: 4th (Carmarthen), 5th (Pontypridd), 6th (Swansea), 7th (Cardiff)

B. Watch: 4th (Dundee), 5th (Arbroath), 6th (Perth), 7th (St. Andrews)

Ox. & Bucks: 4th (Oxford), Buckinghamshire Bn. (Aylesbury)

Essex: 4th (Brentwood), 5th (Chelmsford), 6th (West Ham), 7th (Walthamstow), 8th (Colchester)

Foresters: 5th (Derby), 6th (Chesterfield), 7th (Nottingham), 8th (Newark)

N. Lancs: 4th (Preston), 5th (Bolton)

Northants: 4th (Northampton)

R. Berks: 4th (Reading)

R. W. Kent: 4th (Tonbridge), 5th (Bromley)

KOYLI: 4th (Wakefield), 5th (Doncaster)

KSLI: 4th (Shrewsbury)

Middlesex: 7th (Hornsey), 8th (Hounslow), 9th (Willesden), 10th (Hammersmith)

Wiltshire: 4th (Trowbridge)

Manchester: 5th (Wigan), 6th, 7th (Manchester), 8th (Ardwick), 9th (Ashton), 10th (Oldham)

N. Staffs: 5th (Hanley), 6th (Burton)

Y & L: 4th (Sheffield), 5th (Rotherham)

DLI: 5th (Stockton), 6th (Bishop Auckland), 7th (Sunderland), 8th (Durham), 9th (Gateshead)

HLI: 5th, 6th, 7th (Glasgow), 8th (Lanark), 9th (Glasgow)

Seaforth: 4th (Dingwall), 5th (Golspie), 6th (Elgin)

Gordon: 4th (Aberdeen), 5th (Peterhead), 6th (Keith), 7th (Banchory), Shetland Cos. (Lerwick)

Cameron: 4th (Inverness)

A & SH: 5th (Greenock), 6th (Paisley), 7th (Stirling), 8th (Dunoon), 9th (Dumbarton)

RWF: 4th (Wrexham), 5th (Flint), 6th (Carnarvon), 7th (Newtown)

SWB: Brecknockshire Bn. (Brecon)

KOSB: 4th (Galashiels), 5th (Dumfries)

S.R.: 5th (Glasgow), 6th (Hamilton), 7th, 8th (Glasgow)

Gloster: 4th (Bristol), 5th (Gloucester), 6th (Bristol)

Worcester: 7th (Kidderminster), 8th (Worcester)

E. Lancs: 4th (Blackburn), 5th (Burnley)

E. Surrey: 5th (Wimbledon), 6th (Kingston)

DCLI: 4th (Truro), 5th (Bodmin)

D of Ws: 4th (Halifax), 5th (Huddersfield), 6th (Skipton), 7th (Milnsbridge)

Border: 4th (Carlisle), 5th (Workington)

R. Sussex: 4th (Horsham), 5th (Hastings), 6th (Brighton)

Hampshire: 4th (Winchester), 5th (Southampton), 6th (Portsmouth), 7th (Bournemouth), 8th (Newport), 9th (Southampton)

S. Staffs: 5th (Walsall), 6th (Wolverhampton)

Dorset; 4th (Dorchester)

S. Lancs: 4th (Warrington), 5th (St. Helens)

The new system also introduced independent regiments wholly made up of Territorials, these being the Monmouthshire, Cambridgeshire, Hertfordshire, Herefordshire and London Regiments. The latter, with its 26 battalions, was the largest regiment, Regular or otherwise, in the British Army at the time.

There was also the infantry section of the Honourable Artillery Company; originally intended for the London Regiment as its 26th Battalion, but would have none of this, and remained as it was. Likewise, the Inns of Court Rifles (14th Middlesex Volunteer Rifle Corps) chose to ignore an order directing it to become the 27th Battalion, London Regiment, and instead provided an officers' training unit. Consequently, both the 26th and 27th positions in the

London Regiment remained vacant. There was also a change within the London Regiment in 1912 when its 10th Battalion at Paddington was disbanded, and replaced in the East London Borough of Hackney.

Also new to the British Army, except for the old 26th Middlesex Rifle Volunteer Corps formed in 1888, were a number of battalions completely dedicated to a cyclist role. Most of these were linked to county regiments and were numbered as battalions with the word 'Cyclist' in brackets. Several cyclists battalions were, however, formed and served independently. Independent Territorial regiments and battalions in 1914 were:

HAC, Infantry: (Finsbury)
Monmouthshire Regt: 1st (Newport), 2nd (Pontypool), 3rd (Abergavenny)
Cambridgeshire Regt: 1st (Cambridge)
London Regt: 1st (Bloomsbury), 2nd (Westminster), 3rd (St. Pancras), 4th (Shoreditch), 5th, 6th, 7th, 8th (Finsbury), 9th (Westminster), 10th (Hackney), 11th (Finsbury), 12th (Holborn), 13th (Kensington), 14th, 15th, 16th (Westminster), 17th (Bow), 18th (Chelsea), 19th (Camden Town), 20th (Blackheath), 21st (Camberwell), 22nd (Bermondsey), 23rd (Battersea), 24th (Southwark), 25th (Fulham), 28th (St. Pancras)
Inns of Court OTC: (Lincoln's Inn)
Hertfordshire Regt: 1st (Hertford)
Herefordshire Regt: 1st (Hereford)
Northern Cyclist Bn: (Newcastle)
Highland Cyclist Bn: (Kirkcaldy)
Kent Cyclist Bn: (Tonbridge)
Hunts Cyclist Bn: (Huntingdon)

Eastern (Chelmsford)
Highland (Inverness)
London (Holborn)
Lowland (Edinburgh)
North Midland (Leicester)
1st South Midland (Birmingham)
2nd South Midland (Reading)
Notts and Derby (Chesterfield)
South Eastern (Croydon)
South Wales (Swansea)
1st South Western (Tisbury)
2nd South Western (Weston-super-Mare)
Welsh Border (Birkenhead)
Yorkshire (York)

Army Service Corps

Upon the formation of the Territorial Force, the Army Service Corps (T.F.) was organised into two sections: Mounted Brigade Transport and Supply Columns, and Divisional Transport and Supply Columns. In the case of the former one unit of company strength was provided for each brigade as follows:

2nd Lt. Eric Yarrow, 7th Bn. Argyll and Sutherland Highlanders, killed in action at Frezenberg Ridge on 9 May 1915. Note the Scottish pattern service dress jacket, with the cut-away doublet front allowing space for the sporran, in this case that of the Argylls' pattern, with a badger's head and six tassels.

For the divisions, four companies per column were allotted—one attached to Headquarters and one each to the three infantry brigades within the division. With the exception of the Highland and Lowland Divisions, whose ASC companies had been numbered by 1914, all brigade companies bore the name of the infantry brigade to which they were attached, e.g. Durham Light Infantry Brigade Company, Army Service Corps. Divisional Transport and Supply Columns were as follows:

East Anglian (Ilford)
Highland (Perth)
Home Counties
  (Hounslow)
East Lancashire
  (Manchester)
West Lancashire
  (Southport)
1st London (Plumstead)
2nd London (Chelsea)
Lowland (Glasgow)
North Midland (Leicester)
South Midland (Aston)
Northumbrian
  (Newcastle-upon-Tyne)
West Riding (Leeds)
Welsh (Hereford)
Wessex (Exeter)

1st West Lancashire
  (Liverpool)
2nd West Lancashire
  (Liverpool)
3rd West Lancashire
  (St. Helens)
1st London (Chelsea)
2nd London (Chelsea)
3rd London (Chelsea)
4th London (Woolwich)
5th London (Greenwich)
6th London (Chelsea)
1st Lowland (Glasgow)
2nd Lowland (Glasgow)
3rd Lowland (Edinburgh)
1st North Midland
  (Derby)
2nd North Midland
  (Leicester)
3rd North Midland
  (Wolverhampton)
1st South Midland
  (Birmingham)
2nd South Midland
  (Birmingham)
3rd South Midland
  (Bristol)
1st Northumbrian
  (Newcastle-upon-Tyne)
2nd Northumbrian
  (Darlington)
3rd Northumbrian (Hull)
1st West Riding (Leeds)
2nd West Riding (Leeds)
3rd West Riding
  (Sheffield)
1st Welsh (Ebbw Vale)
2nd Welsh (Cardiff)
3rd Welsh (Swansea)
1st Wessex (Exeter)
2nd Wessex (Plymouth)
3rd Wessex (Portsmouth)

Royal Army Medical Corps

Each of the 14 mounted brigade field ambulances comprised two sections, while divisional field ambulance units, three per division, were made up of three. Mounted Brigade Field Ambulances were:

Eastern (Luton)
Highland (Inverness)
London (Holborn)
Lowland (Glasgow)
North Midland
  (Handsworth)
Notts and Derby
  (Nottingham)
South Eastern (Margate)
1st South Midland
  (Birmingham)
2nd South Midland
  (Stony Stratford)
South Wales (Hereford)
1st South Western
  (Swindon)
2nd South Western
  (Frome)
Welsh Border (Chester)
Yorkshire (Wakefield)

Divisional Field Ambulances:

1st East Anglian (Ipswich)
2nd East Anglian
  (Norwich)
3rd East Anglian
  (Walthamstow)
1st Highland (Aberdeen)
2nd Highland (Aberdeen)
3rd Highland (Dundee)
1st Home Counties
  (Maidstone)
2nd Home Counties
  (Ashford)
3rd Home Counties
  (Surbiton)
1st East Lancashire
  (Manchester)
2nd East Lancashire
  (Manchester)
3rd East Lancashire
  (Manchester)

There were twenty-three General Hospitals attached to the several Commands:

1st Eastern (Cambridge)
2nd Eastern (Brighton)
1st London (Chelsea)
2nd London (Chelsea)
3rd London (Holborn)
4th London (Chelsea)
1st Northern
  (Newcastle-upon-Tyne)
2nd Northern (Leeds)
3rd Northern (Sheffield)
4th Northern (Lincoln)
5th Northern (Leicester)
1st Scottish (Aberdeen)
2nd Scottish (Edinburgh)
3rd Scottish (Glasgow)
4th Scottish (Glasgow)
1st Southern
  (Birmingham)
2nd Southern (Bristol)
3rd Southern (Oxford)
4th Southern (Plymouth)
5th Southern (Gosport)
1st Western (Liverpool)
2nd Western (Manchester)
3rd Western (Cardiff)

Other RAMC units were the 1st and 2nd London Sanitary Companies at Chelsea, and for each division a Clearing Hospital located at:

East Anglian (Ipswich)
Highland (Aberdeen)
Home Counties (Surbiton)
East Lancashire
  (Manchester)
West Lancashire (Kendal)
1st London (Chelsea)
2nd London (Chelsea)
Lowland (Glasgow)
North Midland (Leicester)
South Midland
  (Birmingham)
Northumbrian
  (Newcastle-upon-Tyne)
Welsh (Cardiff)
Wessex (Exeter)
West Riding (Leeds)

Territorial Force Nursing Service

Consisting of trained women, under the command of a Matron-in-Chief, the TFNS provided nursing staff for General Hospitals.

Divisions

The 14 Divisional Areas of the Territorial Force were based on existing Military Districts Numbers 1–10 and London, Numbers 3, 5 and London each being sub-divided into two divisions. Divisions and infantry brigades were named and did not receive numbers until after war was declared. The following order of battle is that for each division just prior to the outbreak of war, and shows infantry brigades with their battalions:

East Anglian Division
Norfolk and Suffolk Bde: (4th, 5th Norfolk, 4th, 5th Suffolk)
East Midland Bde: (5th Beds, 4th Northants, 1st Cambs, 1st Herts)
Essex Bde: (4th, 5th, 6th, 7th Essex)

Highland Division
Seaforth and Cameron Bde: (4th, 5th, 6th Seaforth, 4th Cameron)
Gordon Bde: (4th, 5th, 6th, 7th Gordon)
Argyll and Sutherland Bde: (6th, 7th, 8th, 9th Argyll & Sutherland)

Home Counties Division
Surrey Bde: (4th, 5th R. W. Surrey, 5th, 6th E. Surrey)
Kent Bde: (4th, 5th E. Kent, 4th, 5th R. W. Kent)
Middlesex Bde: (7th, 8th, 9th, 10th Middlesex)

East Lancashire Division
Lancashire Fusiliers Bde: (5th, 6th, 7th, 8th Lancashire Fus.)
East Lancashire Bde: 4th, 5th E. Lancashire, 9th, 10th Manchester)
Manchester Bde: (5th, 6th, 7th, 8th Manchester)

West Lancashire Division
North Lancashire Bde: (4th, 5th R. Lancaster, 4th, 5th N. Lancashire)
Liverpool Bde: (5th, 6th, 7th, 8th Liverpool)
South Lancashire Bde: (9th, 10th Liverpool, 4th, 5th S. Lancashire)

1st London Division
1st London Bde: (1st, 2nd, 3rd, 4th London)
2nd London Bde: (5th, 6th, 7th, 8th London)
3rd London Bde: (9th, 10th, 11th, 12th London)

2nd London Division
4th London Bde: (13th, 14th, 15th, 16th London)
5th London Bde: (17th, 18th, 19th, 20th London)
6th London Bde: (21st, 22nd, 23rd, 24th London)

The badges being worn above the chevrons of these 5th South Staffordshire Regiment NCOs indicate the role that each man plays within his battalion. The brass fleur-de-lys device on the left denotes that the wearer is a 1st Class Scout; while on the right the intertwined letters 'SB' on a disc mark a soldier holding a proficiency certificate in ambulance work. (Chris Coogan)

South Midland Bde: (5th Gloucester, 4th Ox. & Bucks, Bucks Bn, 4th R. Berkshire)

Northumbrian Division
Northumberland Bde: (4th, 5th, 6th, 7th Northumberland
   Fus.)
York and Durham Bde: (4th E. Yorkshire, 4th, 5th
   Yorkshire, 5th DLI)
Durham Light Infantry Bde: (6th, 7th, 8th, 9th DLI)

West Riding Division
1st West Riding Bde: (5th, 6th, 7th, 8th W. Yorkshire)
2nd West Riding Bde: (4th, 5th, 6th, 7th Duke of
   Wellington's)
3rd West Riding Bde: (4th, 5th KOYLI, 4th, 5th York
   & Lancs)

Welsh Division
Cheshire Bde: (4th, 5th, 6th, 7th Cheshire)
North Wales Bde: (4th, 5th, 6th, 7th R. Welsh Fus.)
Welsh Border Bde: (1st, 2nd, 3rd Monmouth,
   1st Hereford)

Wessex Division
Devon and Cornwall Bde: (4th, 5th Devon, 4th, 5th
   DCLI)
South Western Bde: (4th, 5th Somerset LI, 4th Dorset,
   4th Wilts)
Hampshire Bde: (4th, 5th, 6th, 7th Hampshire)

Lt. Col. H. M. Hannan, TD, 8th Bn., The Cameronians (Scottish Rifles), killed in action on 21 June 1915. As Commanding Officer, Lt. Col. Hannan took the 8th Cameronians to Gallipoli in May 1915, where they served as part of 156th Brigade, 52nd (Lowland) Division. This photograph shows the colonel in the full dress of his battalion.

Lowland Division
South Scottish Bde: (4th, 5th RSF, 4th, 5th KOSB)
Scottish Rifle Bde: (5th, 6th, 7th, 8th Cameronians)
Highland Light Infantry Bde: (5th, 6th, 7th, 9th HLI)

North Midland Division
Lincoln and Leicester Bde: (4th, 5th Lincoln, 4th, 5th
   Leicester)
Staffordshire Bde: (5th, 6th S. Stafford, 5th, 6th
   N. Stafford)
Notts and Derby Bde: (5th, 6th, 7th, 8th Notts & Derby)

South Midland Division
Warwickshire Bde: (5th, 6th, 7th, 8th Warwick)
Gloucester and Worcester Bde: (4th, 6th Gloucester,
   7th, 8th Worcester)

The 14 Mounted Brigades each comprised three Yeomanry regiments, one battery (with ammunition column) of horse artillery, a transport and supply column and field ambulance. Yeomanry and RHA units were:

Eastern Mounted Brigade
Suffolk Yeomanry
Norfolk Yeomanry
Essex Yeomanry
Essex RHA

South Eastern Mounted Brigade
East Kent Yeomanry
West Kent Yeomanry
Sussex Yeomanry
B Battery, HAC

London Mounted Brigade
City of London Yeomanry
1st County of London Yeomanry
3rd County of London Yeomanry
A Battery, HAC

Yorkshire Mounted Brigade
Yorkshire Hussars Yeomanry
Yorkshire Dragoons Yeomanry
East Riding Yeomanry
West Riding RHA

1st South Western Mounted Brigade
Royal Wiltshire Yeomanry
North Somerset Yeomanry
Hampshire Yeomanry
Hampshire RHA

2nd South Western
    Mounted Brigade
1st Devon Yeomanry
Royal North Devon
    Yeomanry
West Somerset Yeomanry
Somerset RHA

Welsh Border Mounted
    Brigade
Shropshire Yeomanry
Cheshire Yeomanry
Denbighshire Yeomanry
Shropshire RHA

South Wales Mounted
    Brigade
Pembroke Yeomanry
Montgomery Yeomanry
Glamorgan Yeomanry
Glamorgan RHA

Notts and Derby Mounted
    Brigade
Nottingham Yeomanry
South Notts Hussars
    Yeomanry
Derbyshire Yeomanry
Nottinghamshire RHA

North Midland Mounted
    Brigade
Staffordshire Yeomanry
Leicestershire Yeomanry

Lincolnshire Yeomanry
Leicestershire RHA

Highland Mounted Brigade
Fife and Forfar Yeomanry
1st Lovat's Scouts
    Yeomanry
2nd Lovat's Scouts
    Yeomanry
Inverness-shire RHA

Lowland Mounted Brigade
Ayrshire Yeomanry
Lanarkshire Yeomanry
Lothians and Border
    Horse Yeomanry
Ayrshire RHA

1st South Midland
Mounted
    Brigade
Warwickshire Yeomanry
Gloucestershire Yeomanry
Worcestershire Yeomanry
Warwickshire RHA

2nd South Midland
    Mounted Brigade
Buckinghamshire
    Yeomanry
Berkshire Yeomanry
Oxfordshire Yeomanry
Berkshire RHA

BADGES AND UNIFORM

The only obligatory uniform for officers and men of the Territorial Force was regulation service dress; authorised patterns of full dress were laid down for each unit, but its provision was optional. If and when full dress was to be worn, Territorial Force Regulations clearly set conditions as to its use. Officers' badges of rank were similar to those in the regular army, the letter 'T' being worn on the shoulder cords and straps in full dress uniform. In service dress the 'T' was worn below the collar badges.

A distinction of the Volunteer, and subsequently the Territorial, was the substitution of silver or white metal lace and ornaments for any that were gold or gilding metal in the Regular Army. This was never popular, and the Territorial, it would seem, was not keen to be seen in the public eye as anything less than a Regular. As this rule was likely to affect recruiting the War Office made provisions in TF Regulations for any unit desirous to adopt gold in lieu of silver to seek permission through its County TF Associations. Applications (which required full details of why the unit was requesting permission), once endorsed by the TFAs, would then be passed to the War Office for consideration. Many but by no means all TF units did apply and these requests, which are still on

1st London Divisional Transport and Supply Column, Army Service Corps at camp in 1914. Headquarters of this unit were in Charles Street, Plumstead; and like many other ASC (TF) companies, transport had to be hired from local firms during annual camps. Note special tarpaulin and temporary War Department markings.

Sergeant, 1st North Midland Division Field Ambulance, Royal Army Medical Corps, 1914. This soldier wears above his chevrons the Geneva Cross: a cloth badge comprising, on a black backing, a red cross on a white ground within a yellow circle. He also wears the white metal Imperial Service brooch.

badges. Others were permitted the badges of their parent regiment, but with scrolls etc. that normally displayed battle honours left either plain or inscribed with any distinction that the TF unit possessed. A number of units added additional scrolls to their standard pattern badges, usually bearing the South Africa honour gained by their Volunteer predecessors for service in the Boer War.

Units were easily identified by means of a metal title placed on each shoulder strap. These were worn in both full and service dress, and general regulations as to their construction were published as a special Appendix in TF Regulations. In the main, titles were of a three-tier format, the letter 'T' at the top of the title with arm of service—RHA, RFA, RE, etc.—or battalion number below this. The lower line would then indicate to which regiment a battalion belonged, or in the case of RA, RE units etc., its division or unit. The titles of Yeomanry regiments comprised the letter 'T' over 'Y' over unit name, while those for fusilier and light infantry battalions also incorporated grenades or bugle horns. A small number of battalions also had part of their subsidiary titles incorporated into the shoulder title.

A badge unique to the Territorial Force was a five-pointed star to be worn on the right forearm by other ranks who had been returned as qualified four times. A qualified return was over a period of one year and additional stars were permitted for every further

record, reveal that permission was granted in every case.

The majority of TF infantry full dress uniforms followed the pattern of those worn by the parent regiment. A small number of battalions, however, did have their own distinct style, and continued with the greys and rifle greens that they had worn as Volunteers. The Yeomanry retained its full dress, unique to each regiment, and also provided itself with a special 'substitute' full dress for more ceremonial occasions.

The Yeomanry, independent TF regiments and a small number of battalions wore their own special

Wireless Section, Westmorland and Cumberland Yeomanry, Penrith, c1914. This portable Marconi equipment was provided for the Regiment, at his own expense, by Maj. C. Beddington. Note the officers' jackets with their unique white gorget patches with red central cord.

aggregate of four years. Previous service in the Imperial Yeomanry or Volunteers was taken into consideration, and it is not unusual to see in photographs old Territorials in possession of up to eight stars.

As was the case with the Regular and New Armies, units of the Territorial Force adopted coloured identification patches during the war. Worn on the sleeves, backs of jackets and helmets, this new form of device appeared in many shapes and colours and served to indicate formations, battalions and even companies.

Also worn by Territorials, and unique within the TF, were the Imperial Service brooch, and the cloth badge for members of the Special Service Section.

ORGANISATION 1914–1918

Having volunteered for overseas service, units of the Territorial Force quickly set about the formation of a second line. The intention was that these new formations would take over the role of home defence while at the same time providing and training reinforcements for the original unit. In September 1914 it was decided that 14 new TF divisions would be created out of these second-line personnel. By this time, however, it had been realised that these would be required for active service and men joining would be liable for overseas duty. Subsequently a third line was established which took over the role of recruiting and providing drafts for the first and second lines.

Both second- and third-line units were raised at regimental level and it followed that a system of identification was required. In the case of parent, or first line units, these would be distinguished by the prefix 1/, the second and third lines following on with 2/ and 3/. As an example the pre-war 4th Battalion, Royal Scots became 1/4th, followed by 2/4th and 3/4th.

For the several units that prior to the war bore no numerical designation, such as the Hertfordshire Regiment, these were styled as e.g. 1/1st, 2/1st and 3/1st Battalions, Hertfordshire Regiment. Likewise, the Yeomanry regiments became e.g. 1/1st, 2/1st and

Bedfordshire Yeomanry, 1914. Note the 1903 leather equipment, drab cap-cover, white lanyard, and Imperial Service brooch.

3/1st Yorkshire Hussars. Artillery, engineer, medical and other supporting units similarly received numerical prefixes.

By the end of 1915 third-line reserve battalions were organised into 14 groups, one per pre-war division. Then, in April 1916, the 3/ prefix was dropped and instead battalions became known as e.g. 4th Reserve Battalion, Royal Scots. On 1 September 1916 reserve battalions were reorganised yet again. This time the battalions within a regiment were amalgamated under the number of the senior and, with the exception of some larger regiments that had two, provided a single reserve battalion. At the same time the 14 reserve groups were designated as brigades, assuming divisional titles, e.g. East Anglian Reserve Brigade.

To cater for Territorials unavailable for overseas service, units known as Provisional Battalions were formed in 1915. A number of these were used to make up the new Home Service Divisions—71st, 72nd and 73rd—upon their formation in November 1916. On 1 January 1917 Provisional battalions were placed into regiments, assuming the next available number, which by this time followed on from the New Army battalions.

In May 1915 numbers were allotted to TF divisions according to the order that they went overseas, their pre-war designations being retained in brackets after the number. By this time the formation of the New, or 'Kitchener's' Army had been completed, its divisions having received numbers up to 41. It followed that the original 14 TF divisions, together with their second line, were numbered from 42nd on. These were followed by the formation in 1916 of the three home-service divisions—71st, 72nd, 73rd—and, in Egypt during 1917, by the 74th and 75th. No 70th Division was ever formed.

TF infantry brigades were also numbered, the first being 125th with the remainder following on, e.g. 42nd Division (125th, 126th, 127th Brigades), 43rd Division (128th, 129th, 130th Brigades), etc. A convenient method of determining what brigades were originally allotted to each division is to multiply the number of the division by three: the result gives the number of its middle brigade, e.g. 42nd Division $\times$ 3 = 126. This system, in fact, works from the 7th Division, less 74th and 75th, on, but would not take into account any permanent transfers of brigades from one division to another.

Territorial Divisions

42nd (East Lancashire)	60th (2nd/2nd London)
43rd (Wessex)	61st (2nd South
44th (Home Counties)	Midland)
45th (2nd Wessex)	62nd (2nd West Riding)
46th (North Midland)	63rd (2nd
47th (2nd London)	Northumbrian)
48th (South Midland)	64th (2nd Highland)
49th (West Riding)	65th (2nd Lowland)
50th (Northumbrian)	66th (2nd East
51st (Highland)	Lancashire)
52nd (Lowland)	67th (2nd Home
53rd (Welsh)	Counties)
54th (East Anglian)	68th (2nd Welsh)
55th (West Lancashire)	69th (2nd East Anglian)
56th (1st London)	71st
57th (2nd West	72nd
Lancashire)	73rd
58th (2nd/1st London)	74th (Yeomanry)
59th (2nd North	75th
Midland)	

4th Bn. (Queen's Edinburgh Rifles), The Royal Scots (Lothian Regiment) at camp in 1914. Plain blue glengarries are worn with khaki service dress. Note the Scottish doublet pattern jacket, black buttons and 1908 pattern web belt. The blackened brass shoulder titles are 'T' over '4' over 'QER', over 'ROYAL SCOTS' in an arc.

It will be noticed from the above list that the second line for the Wessex Division was numbered as 45th, its field artillery brigades and ten battalions of infantry having moved to India in December 1914. The 63rd, 64th, 65th, 67th, 68th and 69th Divisions did not go overseas, the former being broken up in July 1916 with its number going to the Royal Naval Division.

Divisional field artillery brigades received Roman numerical designations, starting at CCX (210) in the 42nd, and moving on, with gaps, throughout the divisions. At the same time batteries were lettered within the brigade—'A', 'B', etc. Both field engineer and divisional train companies were numbered.

There were no mounted divisions within the TF prior to the war, but by the end of August 1914 two had been formed from the existing mounted brigades. A 2/2nd Mounted Division was formed in March 1915, and a year later this was renumbered as 3rd. At the same time a 4th was raised in East Anglia, and in June 1917 the Yeomanry Mounted Division was formed in Palestine. Generally, mounted divisions and most second-line Yeomanry regiments were converted to a cyclist role in 1916.

Trench warfare on the Western Front saw the establishment of an infantry division increased by the addition of three (later reduced to two) medium trench mortar batteries, which under the Royal Artillery were lettered as 'X', 'Y' and 'Z'. One heavy mortar battery, lettered as 'V', also formed part of a division between 1916 and 1918. Light trench mortar batteries were the responsibility of the infantry, and these were numbered according to the brigade that they served.

At the beginning of 1916 three companies of machine gunners were formed per division and allotted one to each brigade, being known by the number of their relative brigades. In the following year an additional divisional company was raised and in March 1918 this, along with the MG brigade units,

was merged into a battalion bearing the number of its division.

Other additions to the war-time division were pioneer battalions, mobile veterinary sections and divisional employment companies, all allotted one per division.

WAR SERVICE

In the early months of the war a number of TF battalions went to the front in advance of their peacetime higher formation. One of these, and the first to see action, was the London Scottish, whose gallant attack at Messines on 31 October 1914, where some 43 per cent casualties were sustained, is now a matter of history.

At home the Durham RGA gained the distinction of being the only coast defence unit to be engaged in action during the war, its encounter with the German Navy off Hartlepool on 16 December 1914 also

Drummer Robert Harper, 6th Bn., Gloucestershire Regiment, December 1914. The full dress tunics of this battalion were scarlet with white collars, cuffs and piping. In this photograph note in addition the scarlet wings, white lace with scarlet crowns, and green bugle cords as worn by a drummer. Robert Harper also wears, on the right breast, the Imperial Service brooch, and on the lower left arm two badges for marksmanship—best shot in the band, above best shot in the battalion (junior ranks).

Lance-Corporal, 7th (City of London) Bn., The London Regiment, c1914. This battalion wore scarlet tunics with buff facings in full dress. Note the plain grenade collar badges, and helmet plate bearing the Arms, motto, crossed Mace and Sword of the City of London. (R. J. Marrion)

gaining the first award to any soldier of the Military Medal.

Every unit of the Territorial Force, from the small field company of engineers to the division itself, could justify a written history in its own right; indeed, the services of many divisions and battalions have been published. As the average formation or unit history normally runs to several hundred pages it would be impossible to record here a comprehensive account of service. Instead, mention is made of only the more important movements, battles and engagements at divisional level, with enough detail given, it is hoped, to encourage further study.

42nd (East Lancashire) Division

This division, the first to move overseas, sailed for Egypt in September 1914, its intended role being to take up garrison duty and relieve Regular troops for active service. Having supplied part of the Suez Defence Force, the division saw its first action during the Turkish attack on the Canal in early February 1915.

On 1 May 1915 42nd Div. embarked at Alexandria for Gallipoli, where it was to take part in three important battles: Second Krithia, where the Lancashire Fusiliers of 125th Brigade fought alongside the Regular 29th Division; Third Krithia; and Krithia Vineyard. Subsequent losses of the division at Gallipoli amounted to over 8,000. After the evacuation of Helles during the night of 7/8 January 1916 42nd Div. returned to Egypt, where in the following August two battalions were engaged at Romani.

Orders to leave Egypt for France were received at the end of January 1917, the division arriving in the middle of the following March. After operations on the Flanders Coast and duty in the Ypres Salient, 42nd Div. moved south in March 1918 for action on the Somme, the Germans having commenced their major offensive in that area. Remaining on the Western Front for the rest of the war, 42nd Div. fought in many of the major battles of 1918 — Bapaume, Arras, Ancre, Albert, Canal du Nord and the Selle.

43rd (Wessex) Division

India having consented to send to Europe a number of British Regular and Indian battalions in September 1914, the 43rd was one of several TF divisions that were sent out in exchange. Arriving in November, troops were quickly deployed for garrison duty. The 43rd did not fight as a division; however, in March 1915 the first of the Wessex men moved to the Mesopotamian theatre of war, and in the following September one artillery battery joined the Expeditionary Force in Aden. Units later served in Palestine and took part in the Third Afghan War of May–August 1919.

44th (Home Counties) Division

Early in September 1914 two of the division's

battalions, 7th and 8th Middlesex, left for service in Gibraltar. These were later replaced by 4th Border and 4th KSLI, and the division as a whole left for India on 30 October. During its stay in India the several units of 44th Div. performed garrison duties, while at the same time providing drafts to replace British casualties incurred in Mesopotamia. Various battalions and detachments also served in the Andaman Islands, Aden, Singapore and Hong Kong.

45th (2nd Wessex) Division

This, the first of the TF second-line divisions to go overseas, served in India throughout the war. Numerous drafts and units were also provided for service in Mesopotamia, Aden and Palestine.

46th (North Midland) Division

HM the King inspected the North Midland Division in its Essex war training area on 19 February 1915. Four days later advanced parties were arriving at Boulogne, and by 10 March one battery was in reserve during the Battle of Neuve Chapelle. 139th Brigade having experienced the dreadful liquid-fire attack at Hooge on 30 and 31 July, the division as a whole saw its first major engagement at the Hohenzollern Redoubt—Battle of Loos, 13–15 October.

The 46th was one of the assaulting divisions at the opening of the great Somme offensive on 1 July 1916, working with the 56th (London) Div. in an attack north of the line at Gommecourt. Having suffered heavy casualties during the early hours of 1 July the division was subsequently withdrawn, and did not see any major engagement until the following year.

During the 1917 Advance to the Hindenburg Line 46th Div. were engaged in operations along the Ancre, and played an important role during the attack on Liévin (1 July); part of the division, with Canadians on the right, fought at the Battle of Hill 70 (15–25 August).

No important action was seen by the division during the last year of the war, until 29 September and the great Hindenburg Line battles—St. Quentin Canal, Bellenglise, Beaurevoir Line and Cambrai.

47th (2nd London) Division

Advance parties of the 47th Div. arrived in France during the second week of March 1915, the whole division going into action for the first time at Aubers

Bass-drummer, 2nd Home Counties Field Ambulance, RAMC, c1914.

Ridge on 9 May. The battles of Festubert, Loos (where the Division was on the extreme right of the British Army), and Hohenzollern Redoubt followed during the rest of the year.

The Londoners were holding positions at Vimy Ridge when on 21 May 1916 the enemy attacked, making a small gain in ground. Later, and during the 1916 offensive on the Somme, honours were gained at Flers-Courcelette and Le Transloy.

At Messines on 7 June 1917 the 47th Div., under Maj.-Gen. Sir G. F. Gorringe, were heavily engaged at a German strongpoint known as the White Chateau. After the later stages of the Third Battle of Ypres the division greatly distinguished itself during the Battle of Cambrai, both at the capture of Bourlon Wood and during the subsequent German counterattacks.

4th Bn., The Queen's (Royal West Surrey Regiment) marching through Croydon on its way to war stations in Maidstone, 5 August 1914. Battalion records show that this was a wet day; see rain wear being worn by policemen and the mounted officer on the left. Warmer and drier climates were soon to be experienced; the Battalion left for India, where it was to spend the rest of the war, on 29 October. (D. Barnes)

During the last year of the war the London Territorials took part in the Second Battle of the Somme and the final advance in Artois.

48th (South Midland) Division

After mobilisation this division concentrated around Chelmsford. Orders to move overseas came on 13 March 1915, and by 3 April formation was complete south and east of Cassel.

After just over a year of trench warfare, 48th Div. was to fight in its first large engagement on 1 July 1916, when under the command of Maj.-Gen. R. Fanshawe the division were in corps reserve during the early stages of the Somme offensive. Two of the Warwickshire battalions, however, attacked at 'Zero' with the 4th Division.

Having taken an active part during the March/April 1917 German retreat to the Hindenburg Line, 48th Div. then moved north to the Ypres Salient. Here, during August, September and the first week of October, the 48th formed part of XVIII Corps, and as such were in action at Langemarck, Polygon Wood, Broodseinde and Poelcappelle.

After the early November 1917 reverse in Italy it was decided to send to that theatre a combined force of British and French troops which would include the 48th, overall British commander being Gen. Sir Herbert Plumer. Here the division was involved in the June 1918 fighting on the Asiago Plateau and in November that in the Val d'Assa.

49th (West Riding) Division

The 49th Division served on the Western Front throughout the war, its first major engagement being at Aubers Ridge on 9 May 1915. The following December the Yorkshire men experienced what is now on record as the Germans' first phosgene gas attack.

The year 1916 saw the division in action around the Thiepval area on the first day of the Somme offensive, and later at Bazentin, Pozières and during the first tank attack at Flers-Courcelette on 15 September. The 49th was moved north to the Ypres area in October.

After the 9 October 1917 Battle of Poelcappelle, where the division fought alongside two other Territorial divisions (48th and 66th), the 49th settled down to its second winter in the trenches; the Third Battle of Ypres had died down but casualties remained high due to the enemy's unceasing shellfire.

For the 49th the great April 1918 battles, collectively known as the Battles of the Lys, included Estaires, Messines, Bailleul and Kemmel Ridge. In this period the 49th, along with four other TF divisions, experienced some of the bloodiest fighting of the war, one or other of the three brigades being engaged almost daily.

50th (Northumbrian) Division

This division saw its first action at the Ypres Salient during the April–June 1915 battles at St. Julien, Frezenberg and Bellewaarde. When the fighting began at St. Julien on 24 April some battalions of the 50th Div. had only been in France a matter of days. They were also to experience gas, then being used for the first time in warfare.

Heavily involved during the 1916 Somme offensive, the division then moved north for the 1917 Battles of Arras and Passchendaele. The last year of the war saw the 50th once again in the Somme area and later, during the advance to victory, engaged at the battles of the Hindenburg Line and the Selle and Sambre Rivers.

51st (Highland) Division

For this division mobilisation began on 5 August 1914, and by the 17th its concentration was complete in the Bedford area where training for war commenced. Between 30 April and 3 May the Highlanders crossed to France; by this time one of its brigades comprised battalions that had been transferred from the West Lancashire Division.

Within weeks the 51st Div. saw its first action at Festubert (19–25 May), and then on 15–16 June at Givenchy. During the 1916 Somme offensive the division suffered heavy casualties in attacks on High Wood. It then took part in the capture of Beaumont Hamel, where its splendid memorial can now be seen.

In 1917 the offensive at Arras involved the 51st Div. in fierce fighting around the Scarpe River. Ypres followed, with the division at Pilckem and Menin Road Ridges, and then in November an important part was played during the tank attack, and subsequent capture of Bourlon Wood, at Cambrai.

St. Quentin, Bapaume, Estaires and Hazebrouck all featured in the division's record during the German spring offensive of 1918. The battles of the

10th (Scottish) Bn., The King's (Liverpool Regiment) at Tunbridge Wells, Kent, in October 1914. The Liverpool Scottish arrived at Tunbridge Wells on 10 October and on 2 November were in France as reinforcements for the British Expeditionary Force. Note rolled great coats and drab aprons worn over Forbes tartan kilts. (Brian Nevison)

Marne followed in July, and action was seen during the closing weeks of the war around the Scarpe and Selle Rivers.

52nd (Lowland) Division

On its way to Liverpool, where part of the Lowland Division was embarking for Gallipoli, a train carrying men of the 7th Royal Scots was involved in a tragic accident near Gretna, some 210 losing their lives and over 200 suffering injuries.

After the evacuation of Helles on 7/8 January 1916 the 52nd Div. moved to Egypt where it formed part of the Suez Canal Defences. The invasion of Palestine followed in 1917; and in April of the following year, having been relieved by the 7th (Indian) Div., the division transferred to the Western Front.

Concentrating near Abbeville, where it accustomed itself to conditions in France, the 52nd then moved on to Aire and subsequently to the front line at Vimy. The Second Battles of the Somme and Arras, followed by the action around the Canal du Nord, engaged the division during August and October, and on 11 November positions had been taken up beyond Conde, to the north of the Mons Canal.

53rd (Welsh) Division

When the Welsh Division left Bedford for Gallipoli in July 1915 it did so without its artillery, the gunners being re-armed with 18-pdrs. and 4.5 in. howitzers and eventually sent to France. Having suffered heavy casualties during actions around Suvla the 53rd Div. was then taken to Egypt, where it was rejoined by the artillery.

The fighting in August 1916 to the east of the Suez Canal, and now known as the Battle of Romani, saw 158th Bde. in action alongside the 52nd (Lowland) Division. The invasion of Palestine followed in March 1917, in which the 53rd were heavily engaged through to the capture, and subsequent defence, of Jerusalem in December. By the time of its last battle, at Nablus on 18–21 September 1918, most of the 53rd Div. had been replaced by Indian units, only the artillery and three battalions of the original establishment remaining.

54th (East Anglian) Division

As with the Welsh Division, the divisional artillery of the 54th did not move to Gallipoli, but instead went to France before rejoining in Egypt. After the Suvla landings of August 1915 and subsequent heavy fighting in the area the 54th Div. went to Egypt. Duty on No. 1 Section, Suez Canal Defences followed throughout 1916 and until March of the following year, when as part of Eastern Force the 54th were engaged at the First Battle of Gaza. During the Palestine invasion units of the division were heavily

The first Territorial battalion in action; an artist's impression by Ernest Prater of the London Scottish charging at Messines, 31 October 1914.

1: Sgt., Yorkshire Hussars
2: Cpl., East Riding of Yorks. Yeomanry
3: Lieutenant, Hertfordshire Yeomanry
(4, 5, 6: See Plates commentaries)

A

1: Cpl., 10th Bn., King's (Liverpool Regt.)
2: Sgt. Dmr., 15th Bn., London Regt.

3: Pte., 2nd Bn., London Regt.
(4, 5, 6: See Plates commentaries)

1: Sgt., 1/1st Bn., Cambridgeshire Regt.; France
2: Capt., 1/1st Bn., Monmouthshire Regt.; France
3: Cpl., 1/1st Kent Cyclist Bn.; India
(4, 5: See Plates commentaries)

C

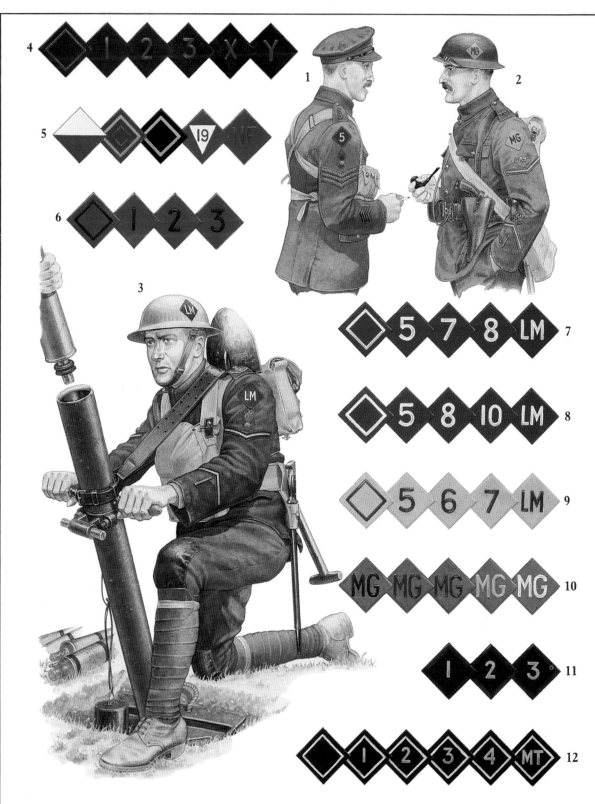

1: Sgt. bomber, 1/5th Bn., Lancs. Fusiliers; France
2: L/Cpl., A Coy., 42nd Bn., MGC; France

3: L/Cpl., 126th Bde. LTM Bty.; France
(4-12: See Plates commentaries)

D

1: Pte., 2/10th Bn., Royal Scots; Russia

2: Pte., 1/6th Bn., HLI; Gallipoli

3: Sniper, 1/24th Bn., London Regt.; France

(4-6: See Plates commentaries)

E

1: Principal Matron, TFNS
2: Cpl., 48th Div. Coy., Army Cyclist Corps
(3-8: See Plates commentaries)

1: 1/1st Welsh Horse; Suez
2, 3: 1/12th Bn., London Regt.; France
(4–10: See Plates commentaries)

G

2

3

4 LONDON IRISH 2/8 L R

LONDON SCOTTISH

5

6

7

9

8

10

WESTMLD & CUMBLD YEOMANRY

1: Pte., 1/14th Bn., London Regt; France
(2-6: See Plates commentaries)

7: Pte., 1/5th Bn., Royal Warwickshire Regt.; Italy
(8-10: See Plates commentaries)

engaged and have been noted for their involvement in numerous actions: one such was the hard fighting by the 1/4th and 1/5th Norfolks at the capture of the strongly fortified position at El Arish.

55th (West Lancashire) Division

The wartime history of the 55th Div. began with a number of its units being withdrawn and sent to reinforce the British Expeditionary Force in France. With eight battalions leaving England between November 1914 and March 1915, and the transfer to other divisions of the remaining units in April, the West Lancashire Division had almost ceased to exist.

The Army Council authorised the reformation of the 55th Div. in November 1915, its original battalions and artillery rejoining and assembling around Hallencourt. The 55th remained on the Western Front for the rest of the war, fighting on the Somme during September 1916, at Ypres and Cambrai in 1917, and throughout the German offensive of April 1918.

56th (1st London) Division

The 1st London Division was another formation that, as a division, took no part in the early stages of the war, its units being used to reinforce the BEF in France and relieve the regular garrison at Malta. Having been reformed in France on 7 January 1916, however, 56th Div. later formed part of the line on the first day of the Somme Offensive, attacking in the north at Gommecourt.

After fighting through the Somme campaign until the actions at the Transloy Ridges in October 1916, the Londoners were at Arras, Ypres and Cambrai during 1917. The last year of the war saw heavy casualties at Arras in March and, after re-entering the line in August, action on the Somme and Hindenburg Line.

57th (2nd West Lancashire) Division

This, the first of the second-line Territorial divisions to move to France, saw its first action at the Battle of Passchendaele, 26 October–7 November 1917. Operations around Arras and the Hindenburg Line followed in 1918, ending with the occupation of Lille on 17 October.

58th (2nd/1st London) Division

Having left for France in January 1917, the 58th Div. were in time to take part in the German retreat to the Hindenburg Line during the following March. At Ypres the division fought gallantly at Menin Road Ridge, Polygon Wood and the second battle of Passchendaele, and in 1918 on the Somme and during the final advance in Artois and Flanders.

59th (2nd North Midland) Division

The 59th was the first Territorial division to serve in Ireland and was involved in the suppression of the Dublin rising during 1916. After war training at Curragh, 59th Div. moved back to England and subsequently to France, where it arrived in time to play an active role during the German spring retreat of 1917. Ypres followed in September, and Cambrai in November and December.

Wounded Belgian troops convalescing in England under the care of women of the Territorial Force Nursing Service. Note the letter 'T' worn at each point of the cape. (Brian Nevison)

Private A. F. Kemp, 1/19th (County of London) Battalion, The London Regiment (St. Pancras), which served with 141st Brigade, 47th Division; he was killed in the Ypres sector on 1 January 1917. The 47th divisional history records that on that day the whole divisional front was subject to a heavy enemy bombardment, causing great damage to the trenches. Note the battalion's dark green 'club' sign, and the brass shoulder title 'T' over 'LONDON'. The brass cap badge of the 19th London Regiment comprised a Maltese cross within a crowned wreath. (Paul Reed)

After the German offensive of March and April 1918 it was necessary, due to extremely high casualties, to reduce units of the division to training cadres. Later 59th Div. was reconstituted and its infantry provided by New Army battalions.

60th (2nd/2nd London) Division

After five months' service in France, which included trench and crater fighting at Vimy Ridge, the 60th Div. received orders to move to Macedonia. Here it assembled at Salonika on Christmas Day 1916, and by 24 April 1917 was involved in the battle at Doiran. In June 1917 the 60th Div. joined the Egyptian Expeditionary Force for service in Palestine, where in December it played an important role during the capture, and subsequent defence, of Jerusalem

61st (2nd South Midland) Division

The 61st Div. saw its first major action in France during an attack, along with Australian troops, at Fromelles on 19 July 1916. In 1917 it took part in operations along the Ancre River, and played an active role during the German retreat of March/April, followed by the Third Battle of Ypres.

For its courageous service during the March 1918 German offensive 61st Div. was frequently mentioned in despatches, coming out of the battle with a splendid reputation. The April, and second, stage of the enemy's spring push also saw the 61st heavily engaged, this time fighting gallantly at Estaires, Hazebrouck and Bethune.

62nd (2nd West Riding) Division

The 62nd Div. crossed to France in January 1917 and in its first year of war saw action in V Corps, Fifth Army area throughout February, March, April, May; and as part of IV Corps, Third Army at Cambrai in the following November. In 1918 the division fought on the Somme, in the battles of the Marne, at Arras and on the Hindenburg Line.

63rd (2nd Northumbrian) Division

By March 1916 the division's strength was some 5,000 below establishment, and this was reduced even further when its artillery left to join the Royal Naval Division in France. With even more men leaving as drafts for first-line units overseas, it was decided to break up the 63rd Div., its number being taken over by the Royal Naval Division on 19 July 1916.

64th (2nd Highland) Division

Served as a home defence formation.

65th (2nd Lowland) Division

Served as a home service formation and disbanded in January 1918.

66th (2nd East Lancashire) Division

The division received its embarkation orders on 11 February 1917, and by 16 March concentration was complete in France under XI Corps, First Army. After duty along the Flanders coast the 66th was relieved by the first-line East Lancashire division, the

42nd. The 66th then moved to the Ypres battle area where, on 9 October, it took part in the action at Poelcappelle and was subsequently mentioned in despatches.

The 66th was again mentioned, and its name linked with 'exceptional gallantry', during the German offensive of March 1918. During this overwhelming attack the men of the division fought at St. Quentin, in the actions at the Somme crossings and at Rosières.

67th (2nd Home Counties) Division, 68th (2nd Welsh) Division, 69th (2nd East Anglian) Division, 71st Division, 72nd Division, and 73rd Division all served solely as home defence formations.

74th (Yeomanry) Division

As a result of Egyptian Expeditionary Force Order No. 26 of 14 January 1917 the dismounted 2nd, 3rd and 4th Brigades of Yeomanry were converted to 229th, 230th and 231st Infantry Brigades. These formations were, the following February, organised as the 74th (Yeomanry) Division and as such fought through to April in Palestine. Having received orders to transfer to France the 74th Div. began to arrive at Marseille on 7 May. It went into the line at Merville in July, and subsequently took part in the Second Battle of Bapaume and Epehy.

75th Division

The last of the Territorial divisions, the 75th, was formed in 1917 and comprised both British and Indian troops. As part of the Egyptian Expeditionary Force the division fought at the Third Battle of Gaza in October/November 1917, and in 1918 at Tell 'Asur, Berukin and Sharon.

1/6th Bn., Durham Light Infantry, in the Ypres Salient on 20 May 1915. This Bishop Auckland battalion moved with the 50th (Northumbrian) Division to France in April 1915 and was committed to hard fighting less than a month later. Four days after this photograph was taken the battalion was involved in the Battle of Bellewaarde Ridge, an assault by the enemy that included the heaviest gas attack yet sustained. Note the primitive gas respirators worn round the neck. (Durham Light Infantry Museum)

THE PLATES

A1: Sergeant, Signals Instructor, Yorkshire Hussars

Full dress was retained by this regiment more than by most others, photographs showing it being worn at church parades and camps as well as on ceremonial occasions. Dating from 1794, and styled as Hussars since 1819, the Yorkshire Hussars wore dark blue jackets and overalls decorated with silver or white cord and lace, the typical hussar-style jacket having, in the case of the sergeants' uniform, 18 rows of double silver cord across the chest. Worn at the front of the busby by other ranks was the Rose of York, the Regiment's badge until 1864 when the title 'Princess of Wales's Own' was conferred and the Plumes, Coronet and Motto introduced. After this the officers' busby badge became the Plumes and later headdress badges combined Plumes and Rose. Worn above the chevrons until 1900, when it was placed on them, the sergeants' arm badge can be seen on the right sleeve, together with the crossed flags (above the chevrons) of a Signals Instructor. Also seen on this uniform are four worsted five-pointed stars, indicat-

ing that the wearer has been returned as qualified four times per star.

In 1914 the Regiment's four squadrons were located at Leeds, York, Knaresborough and Middlesbrough. It subsequently crossed to France and served on the Western Front throughout the war, its last year of service being as part of the 9th West Yorkshire Regiment.

A2: Corporal, East Riding of Yorkshire Yeomanry

Styled as lancers and from Hull, Beverley, Fulford and Driffield, the East Riding Yeomanry wore a combination of two colours described as maroon, or dark scarlet, and French grey (light blue). The forage cap illustrated has the French grey piping arranged in 'lancer' style—viz. around the top of the band, with four vertical lines dividing the crown into quarters. The regimental badge, a fox in full cry with motto 'Forrard', originated from the fact that much of the Regiment was drawn from among the fox-hunting landowners and farmers of the East Riding. The motto, which is also of hunting origin, was not added to the cap and collar badges until 1912.

The East Riding of Yorkshire Yeomanry went to Egypt in October 1915, and subsequently served in Palestine and on the Western Front.

A3: Lieutenant, Hertfordshire Yeomanry

Styled as dragoons, the Hertfordshire Yeomanry wore white metal helmets with black plumes and gilt fittings, the plate bearing, from the County Arms, the device of a hart crossing a ford. The officers' tunics were made from scarlet cloth, collars and cuffs being white and the lace and cord silver, badges of rank being carried on silver plaited shoulder cords. The red leather pouch belt, just over 2 in. wide, was decorated with two strips of silver herringbone wire embroidery, and is completed by, at the back, a black leather and silver pouch, and at the front by a silver rosette, chains and pickers. Trousers/overalls are dark blue with a double scarlet stripe.

Rifleman, 5th (City of London) Bn., The London Regiment (London Rifle Brigade), c1915. According to its regimental history the battalion, in July 1915, introduced embroidered cloth patches (green 'L.R.B.' on a black ground) as a replacement for the blackened brass shoulder title 'T' over '5' over 'CITY OF LONDON'. However, both patterns are seen here being worn simultaneously. (Mike Ingrey)

A4, A5, A6: Full dress helmets and cap badge

The headdress shown as A4 is that of the Lincolnshire Yeomanry and typical of that worn by officers of lancer regiments: note the quartered top, high cock's-feather plume, and triangular plate bearing the Arms of Lincoln. At A5 is the unique helmet of the Norfolk Yeomanry with its black leather body, gilt fittings and yellow plume. For the cap badge of the Berkshire Yeomanry (A6) the skeletal shape of a white horse was chosen, from the ancient chalk figure cut into the downs above Uffington. Also commemorating part of Berkshire was the Regiment's collar badge depicting the crescent and star from the seal of Hungerford.

Lord Radnor, Commanding Officer 1/4th Bn., Wiltshire Regiment, at Delhi in May 1915. Jacob Radnor, the 6th Earl, was a pre-war Volunteer and Territorial, taking over command of his battalion in 1903. He had served in South Africa, and while in India became brigadier-general of the Dehra Dun Brigade. Note the battalion's dark green cross pattée helmet flash.

B1: Corporal, 10th (Scottish) Battalion, The King's (Liverpool Regiment)

Formed as the 8th Volunteer Battalion, King's (Liverpool Regiment) in 1900 from Scots living in and around Liverpool, the 10th King's wore a uniform that included drab doublets and Forbes pattern kilts. A glengarry with black cock's feathers, scarlet facings, and brown belts made the outfit unique within the British Army. Note the White Horse badge of the King's Regiment worn on the collar and sporran, and the waist belt clasp that still bears the pre-1908 Volunteer designation. The Liverpool Scottish had their headquarters in the City at No. 7 Fraser Street. Both the 1/10th and 2/10th Battalions served on the Western Front throughout the war, the original unit with 9th and 55th Divisions, while the second line formed part of 57th and later 55th. Note the doublet shoulder strap of the Liverpool Scottish shown in detail.

B2: Sergeant, Corps of Drums, 15th (County of London) Bn., The London Regiment (Prince of Wales's Own Civil Service Rifles)

The Civil Service Rifles dates from 1860 when a number of Government departments formed Volunteer corps. With the Prince of Wales as its Hon. Colonel, the Battalion included companies formed from staff at the offices of the Post Office, Inland Revenue, and even the Admiralty. Once again a uniform unique to its unit is illustrated, the Battalion retaining its grey with blue facings from the Volunteer days. As a drummer the Sergeant wears on his shoulders grey wings with blue lace. He also wears a drum above his chevrons, which like his other arm badges is made from silver wire on a blue backing. Note the three 'qualified' badges worn on the lower right arm. Crossed rifles with star above, lower left arm, indicates that the wearer is 'the best marksman' in his squadron, company, or in this case band. Note also the shoulder title of the 15th Londons shown in detail.

From its headquarters at Somerset House in the Strand, the Battalion moved to training areas in Hertfordshire when war was declared. It later crossed to France where it served for the remainder of the war as part of 140th Brigade, 47th Division.

B3: Private, 2nd (County of London) Bn., The London Regiment (Royal Fusiliers)

This battalion's association with the Royal Fusiliers dates from 1873 when as the 46th Middlesex Rifle Volunteer Corps it was linked with the old 7th Foot as part of No. 49 Sub-District Brigade. In its blue-faced scarlet uniforms, the Battalion is typical of many that appeared much the same as their parent regiments, being only identified in most cases by the designation worn on the shoulder strap. Note the full dress fur cap, with grenade badge, as worn by fusilier regiments, the white hackle of the Royal Fusiliers being worn on the right side. Also seen in this illustration is the Special Service Section badge comprising three 'Ss' within a crowned circle. Note also the shoulder title of the 2nd Londons shown in detail.

In 1914 headquarters of the 2nd London Regiment were at Tufton Street in Westminster. Soon after war was declared it assumed its first wartime duty: guarding the railway between Southampton Docks and Amesbury. On 4 September 1914 the Battalion

Men of the 1/4th Northamptonshire Regiment in trenches at Gallipoli. Several dummies have been constructed from surplus items of uniform: in the records of one battalion that served at Gallipoli mention is made of such models being used to draw, and subsequently locate, sniper fire. It is also noted that during the evacuation of the Peninsula in early January 1916 dummies were positioned in the trenches to fool the enemy.

sailed to Malta, but in March of the following year moved to France where it served with the 8th and 56th Divisions.

B4, B5, B6: Badge details

Some of the Territorial Force infantry baattalions that formed part of a line regiment had their own special and individual badges. The Cross of St. Andrew, together with the King's Liverpool's white horse, firmly establishes the Scottish connection of the Regiment's 10th Battalion (B4): this is the badge being worn in the glengarry of B1. Also from Scotland is the crest (a cat-a-mountain) and motto ('Sans Peur'—Without Fear) of the Sutherland family, the badge of the old 1st Sutherland Rifle Volunteers, and from 1908, the 5th Bn., Seaforth Highlanders (B5). A unique feature of this silver officers' badge was the inclusion of feathers to denote rank, i.e. subaltern (one), captain (two), field officer (three), colonel (four). Finally, at B6 we show the black Maltese cross of the Buckinghamshire Battalion, Oxfordshire and Buckinghamshire Light Infantry, its central device being the Swan from the County Arms.

C1: Sergeant, 1/1st Cambridgeshire Regiment; France, 1918

The sergeant wears the 1908 pattern webbing with leather pistol case and ammunition pouch; note

lanyard attached to the butt of the Webley Mk III pistol and worn around the neck. A battalion patch, in the regimental colours of light blue with central black bar, is worn together with three blue overseas service chevrons, the crossed flags of a regimental signaller, and the gold stripes for two wounds.

The Battalion left its headquarters in Corn Exchange Street, Cambridge, just after war began and was soon training in Suffolk. In February 1915 the Cambridgeshires left their own East Anglian Division and joined 82nd Brigade, 27th Division in France. Later service was as a training battalion for 3rd Army School, and then active service with the 39th and 12th Divisions. The cap badge and shoulder title of the Cambridgeshire Regiment are shown in detail.

C2: Captain, 1/1st Battalion, Monmouthshire Regiment; Belgium, 1915

Based on a painting by Fred Roe, this illustration shows an officer in action during the Battle of Frezenberg Ridge, Ypres, on 8 May 1915, where some 21 officers and 439 other ranks were lost. All three first-line battalions of the Monmouthshire Regiment suffered heavy casualties throughout the May fighting around Ypres, and were subsequently amalgamated under the title of The Monmouthshire Regiment. Note the silhouette of a black dragon below the collar, and (in detail) the 1908 pattern webbing worn by some officers in lieu of the Sam Browne, binoculars, ashplant and Webley Mk IV pistol.

C3: Corporal, 1/1st Kent Cyclist Battalion; India, 1917

From Tonbridge the 1st Kent Cyclist Battalion served on coast defences until February 1916 when it sailed for India. For a helmet patch the Battalion chose a cloth version of its cap badge—the White Horse and motto ('Invicta') of Kent. During its service in India the Battalion, having been converted to an infantry role, produced special shoulder titles comprising the number 'I' over 'KENT', these being made locally from cast brass: note both shown in detail. Note also medal ribbons for service in South Africa affixed by a pin-fastener, and chevrons which were attached by press-studs; these items, and other insignia, had to be removed before washing. The khaki drill jacket is known as the 'second pattern', differing from the earlier pre-war version by its rectangular, instead of pointed, pocket flaps.

C4, C5: Badge details

Comprising both Artillery and Infantry sections, the Honourable Artillery Company had its own version of the RA gun badge together with a grenade device based on that of the Grenadier Guards (C4). Note also the 'HAC' shoulder title of the Regiment, this being worn below either 'A' or 'B' by the two artillery batteries. A badge based on that of the Black Watch was worn by the Highland Cyclists (C5); this is shown beside one of the several patterns of shoulder title worn by battalions of the unit.

D1: Sergeant Bomber, 1/5th Bn. Lancashire Fusiliers; France, 1918

To indicate the sergeant's role within his battalion a worsted grenade badge is worn above the chevrons— red flames, khaki ball. His special pouches containing ten Mills bombs are worn at the front; and his flash of a white number on a red ground shows that his battalion was part of 125th Brigade. The metal shoulder titles of battalions forming part of a fusilier regiment also incorporated a grenade; the extra length of this type of title often caused them to snap in the middle, however, as a result of equipment being carried on the shoulder, and it is not unusual to see in photographs broken or just parts of titles being worn. The 5th Lancashire Fusiliers were from Bury. Note the maximum (one red and four blue) overseas service chevrons.

D2: Lance Corporal, A Company, 42nd Bn. Machine Gun Corps; France, 1918

The 42nd Division's machine gun battalion comprised HQ and four companies each with its own

Officers, 1/4th Bn., The Duke of Wellington's (West Riding Regiment), at Fleurbaix in summer 1915. The Germans had first used gas in April 1915 and these three officers— including (centre) Capt. Hugh Stanton of the Royal Scots, and Adjutant to the 1/4th, and (right) Capt. A. L. Mowat—are seen wearing the 'Hypo helmet', an early form of protection against this new weapon. Capt. Mowat, later Lt. Col. Sir Alfred Mowat, DSO, MC and Bar, commanded the battalion from June 1918 to June 1919. (Stuart Barr)

cloth arm patch. Note the lance corporal's white on khaki worsted Machine Gunner's badge, Range-Finder's badge, and Good Conduct chevron. Equipment is the 1914 leather issue including open holster for .45 Webley pistol. Divisional devices were usually painted on the sides of steel helmets in the 42nd Division.

D3: Lance Corporal, 126th Brigade Light Trench Mortar Battery; France, 1918

Light trench mortar batteries (each of eight 'guns') were allotted one per brigade and made up from personnel supplied from within the brigade. In the 42nd Division LTMBs wore the letters 'LM' on a ground of their brigade colour. Part of 126th Brigade was the Oldham unit, the 10th Manchesters, and this battalion wore the usual three-tier metal shoulder title, but with the word 'MANCHESTER' solid instead of the usual pierced style. As a mortar 'No. 1' the lance corporal is seen handling the Stokes mortar. He wears the blue worsted grenade badges of a trench mortarman, a wound stripe, and the Good Conduct chevron for more than two years' service. Note the

General Service wagon of the 50th (Northumbrian) Division just behind the divisional forward area at Mont des Cats in April 1916. Manned by two members of the 1/8th Bn., Durham Light Infantry, *the wagon displays the red unicorn head sign of the 50th Division, this device being the crest of the division's commander Maj. Gen. Percival Wilkinson. (Durham Light Infantry Museum)*

handles and sling on the mortar, replacing a bipod for the attack.

D4–D12: Formation signs

The shape of the 42nd Division sign was a diamond divided white over red, and this would appear on vehicles, sign boards, etc. A basic colour scheme was used to denote arm of service and brigades, the units within each having their own identification within the diamond. The patches shown were worn on the upper arm and represent the divisional order of battle after February 1918.

The first group of patches (D4), from left to right, are the six Royal Artillery signs—RAHQ, the 210th and 211th Brigades with numbers 1 and 2, the ammunition column with the number 3, and the two trench mortar batteries X and Y. At (D5) are the 42nd Division, DHQ HQ Staff, 19th Mobile Veterinary Section, 239th Divisional Employment Company, and the pioneer battalion, 1/7th Northumberland Fusiliers. The three field companies RE were numbered in order of seniority, their headquarters having the first sign shown at (D6).

The next three groups of patches show the division's three infantry brigades, each with its own colours. HQs wore a diamond within a diamond while the battalions had their numbers. Light trench mortar batteries were identified by the letters 'LM'. (D7) 125th Bde.—white on red: 1/5th, 1/7th, 1/8th Lancashire Fusiliers. (D8) 126th Bde.—white on

Sergeant, 3/1st Surrey Yeomanry (Queen Mary's Regiment), at Canterbury in May 1916, in field service marching order. The sergeant's equipment includes the extra four bandolier pouches, issued to and worn on the back by cavalry units. Attached to the sword scabbard are a picketing post and canvas watering bag.

green: 1/5th East Lancs, 1/8th, 1/10th Manchester. (D9) 127th Bde.—red on yellow: 1/5th, 1/6th, 1/7th Manchester.

The machine gunners (D10) wore a light blue diamond with the letters 'MG' coloured according to company—left to right, HQ, A, B, C and D Companies—while the three RAMC field ambulances were numbered (D11). The last group of formation signs (D12) are those of the Army Service Corps—HQ, the four divisional companies numbered, and the motor transport company.

E1: Private, 2/10th (Cyclist) Battalion, The Royal Scots (Lothian Regiment); North Russia, 1918

One of the first units to be sent to North Russia in the summer of 1918 was the 2/10th Royal Scots, who by that time had long ceased to be cyclists and were all men of low medical category. They were armed with the Russian 7.62 Mosin-Nagant model 1891 rifle; and during the winter of 1918/19 were clothed as shown, in outfits devised by the polar explorer Ernest Shackleton (then a major with the North Russia Force). Shown in detail are the 'Polar Star' sign worn on service dress sleeves by the 2/10th Royal Scots and other infantry units in North Russia, and the shoulder title of the battalion.

E2: Private, 1/6th Battalion, The Highland Light Infantry; Gallipoli, 1915

At a time when all other battalions of the HLI wore trews, two Territorial battalions of the Regiment wore the kilt: the 6th (City of Glasgow) and the 9th (Glasgow Highland) Battalions. In the heat of Gallipoli men of the 1/6th HLI were photographed performing what the British Army is pleased to call 'fatigues' in the dress illustrated. Note the kilt-shaped flash of Mackenzie tartan worn on the topi, and the shoulder title of the 6th HLI shown in detail.

E3: Sniper, A Company, 1/24th Battalion, The London Regiment; France

The subject of this illustration is from the South London unit—1/24th (County of London) Bn., The London Regiment (The Queen's). His battalion sign was a red spade, and his company is identified by the blue bar below. As a battalion sniper a green band is worn around the left cuff. Note sleeveless goatskin coat, woollen cap 'comforter', and extra 50-round cotton bandoliers. The telescopic sight fixed to the short Lee Enfield rifle is the Aldis Brothers No. 3.

E4: Arm flashes for 161st Brigade, 54th (East Anglian) Division: left to right—1/4th, 1/5th, 1/6th, 1/7th Battalions, Essex Regiment. Violet portion is worn to the front on both arms.

E5: Shoulder titles

Many units of the time retained the traditions of rifle regiments dating from Rifle Volunteer days; these included the 4th and 5th (Queen's Edinburgh Rifles) Battalions of the Royal Scots, and the 7th and 8th (Leeds Rifles) Battalions of the West Yorkshire

Regiment. We illustrate the shoulder titles for the 4th QER and the 7th Leeds Rifles.

E6: 46th Division insignia

In the 46th (North Midland) Division unit flashes were worn centrally on the back of the jackets, below the collar, by other ranks. Those illustrated are (top to bottom) 1/1st Monmouths, the divisional pioneers; 1/5th North Staffords, other battalions of the 137th Brigade wearing the Staffordshire Knot in red, blue or yellow; 138th Brigade wore symbols in yellow, that for the 1/4th Leicesters being shown; 139th Brigade's battalions were all Sherwood Foresters—their devices were in green, as illustrated by that of the 1/7th Battalion. Officers wore a different scheme of insignia.

F1: Principal Matron, Territorial Force Nursing Service

Rank was indicated by bands of scarlet braid on the cuff—two on each arm for principal matrons, one for matrons. Sisters had one row of narrow scarlet piping

Some officers of the 1/5th Bn., King's (Liverpool Regiment) serving with 165th Bde., 55th Div., in the line at Givenchy in March 1918. Note respirators carried in the 'alert' position; and the three signal rockets behind the officer second left. 1/5th King's held positions at Givenchy at the time of the April 1918 German offensive—the Battle of the Lys.

Divisional Headquarters Staff, 55th (West Lancashire) Division at Auchel in April 1918. (Back row) Maj. R. P. Power, OBE; Capt. R. L. Dobell; Rev. J. O. Coop, DSO; Maj. Sir E. H. Preston, Bart., DSO, MC; Maj. Hon. E. C. Lascelles, DSO, MC. (Front row) Maj. M. H. Milner, DSO, MVO; Lt. Col. S. H. Eden, CMG, DSO; Maj. Gen. Sir H. S. Jeudwine, KCB; Lt. Col. T. R. C. Price, CMG, DSO; Capt. G. Surtees, MC. Note the divisional sign, the Red Rose of Lancaster, on the boards and worn as arm-bands by the officers.

on the right sleeve only. Large white metal 'T's were worn at the points of the cape, and a special silver badge was suspended from a red ribbon with white central stripe (see F4). Note the blue–grey straw bonnet worn when off duty.

F2: Corporal, 48th (South Midland) Divisional Company, Army Cyclist Corps

This unit was administered by the Gloucestershire Territorial Force Association and moved to France at the end of March 1915. Note the 'T' over 'CYCLIST' cloth shoulder title, cyclists' arm badge, and Imperial Service brooch worn on the right breast.

F3: Hampshire Aircraft Parks, Royal Flying Corps

This unique unit was formed from members of the Royal Aircraft Factory at South Farnborough in November 1915. Although part of the Royal Flying Corps, the men wore Army service dress with RFC cloth arm titles and cap badges.

F4: TFNS silver badge

F5: Brass shoulder title worn by the Notts and Derby Mounted Brigade Transport and Supply Column, ASC.

F6: Brass shoulder title worn by 2nd West Riding Brigade, RFA. The remaining three brigades of the division had similar titles but with the relevant number.

F7: Warwickshire RHA cap badge

F8: Left to right—sleeve titles for the Poplar and Stepney Rifles (17th County of London Regt.), and the Artist's Rifles (28th County of London Regt.). Battle patches for the 58th Divisional Engineers; 2/3rd East Lancashire Field Ambulance, RAMC, 66th Division; 146th Light Trench Mortar Battery, 49th Division; and 198th Light Trench Mortar Battery, 66th Division.

G1: 1/1st Welsh Horse Yeomanry; Suez, 1916

Headquarters of the Welsh Horse were at first located in Cardiff, moving to Newtown, Montgomeryshire, shortly after formation. After training in East Anglia the Regiment moved overseas in September 1915, its subsequent service being in Gallipoli, Egypt, France and Flanders. The regimental badge of a leek and the letters 'WH' were displayed on the sides of the foreign service helmet and also above the chevrons of sergeants. Note also the white-on-green arm flash, and the Regiment's unique shoulder title.

G2, G3: 1/12th (County of London) Bn., The London Regiment (The Rangers)

The Rangers moved to France in December 1914 and later served with the 28th, 56th and 58th Divisions. A rifleman of the battalion is seen, 1917, observing the enemy with the aid of a mirror fixed to his bayonet. Note his cloth arm title 'RANGERS' worn in conjunction with a blackened metal version on the shoulder strap; and the red battalion patch, part of the divisional scheme for the 56th Division. The badge of the battalion was a black Maltese cross, and this was worn by officers on the back of the tunics and helmets, as shown.

G4: Battalion signs, West Yorkshire Regiment Territorials

The four first-line battalions wore the letter 'T' in different colours—left to right, 1/5th–1/8th. For the second-line circles were chosen—left to right, 2/5th–2/8th. The signs were worn on the upper arms and were part of the schemes of the 49th and 62nd Divisions.

G5: Unit signs, 61st Division

The shapes selected and worn on the upper arms by the three brigades were: 182nd a square, 183rd a triangle, and 184th a circle. Within the first two brigades the four battalions wore red, blue, yellow, and black in order of seniority, while the machine gun company and light trench mortar battery had green and purple–pink respectively. For 184 Brigade, however, their battalion colours were arranged in a different order, viz. yellow, red, black, light blue. Signs shown are, left to right—2/5th Royal Warwicks, 2/6th Gloucesters and 2/5th Gloucesters, 182nd MGCoy. and 2/8th Worcesters.

G6: Battalion sign, 1/4th Royal Scots Fusiliers, 52nd Division

Worn around the right cuff of jackets in 1918.

G7: Battalion sign, 5th North Staffordshire Regiment, 59th Division

Worn on the sleeves from January until May 1918.

G8: Battalion sign, 1/7th Durham Light Infantry

Worn on sleeves when serving as pioneer battalion to the 8th Division, green disc to the front.

G9: Battalion sign, 2/12th London Regiment

Worn on the sleeves in the 58th Division.

Signaller A. Parry, 2/15th (County of London) Bn., The London Regiment (Prince of Wales's Own, Civil Service Rifles), 1918/1919. The Civil Service Rifles was formed from members of various Government departments, with headquarters at Somerset House in London. After becoming part of 90th Bde., 30th Div., 2/15th Londons assumed that division's formation sign, the crest of its founder Lord Derby: a white swan and heraldic cap on a black disc. Note also the red–orange on khaki title 'CIVIL SERVICE RIFLES'; and the signallers' badge. (Paul Reed)

G10: Battalion sign, 1/7th Middlesex Regiment

Worn on the sleeves in 56th Division until 1917.

H1: Private, 1/14th (County of London) Battalion, The London Regiment (London Scottish); France, 1917

Just visible under the apron is the Regiment's Hodden grey kilt, its other (blue) distinction showing in the Tam O'Shanter tourie, badge backing, and hose top flashes. When steel helmets were issued in March 1916 a small blue tourie was attached to the left side of the khaki cover; this was later discarded—it presented a good aiming mark to the enemy. The two-line brass shoulder title 'LONDON/SCOTTISH' (see detail) was introduced in 1915, replacing the usual three-tier type. A red inverted triangle was worn by the 'Scottish' after joining 168th Brigade, 56th Division in February 1916. Note the 1908 pattern field service marching order webbing, Hodden grey hose tops, and the London Scottish tactical sign.

H2: 3rd (Reserve) (City of London) Bn., The London Regiment (Royal Fusiliers)

Brass shoulder titles incorporating a grenade and the letters 'RF' were worn together with the cloth pattern (red letters on khaki) after the Battalion was redesignated from 4/3rd London Regiment in April 1916.

H3: 1/1st Shropshire Yeomanry

Photographs taken of the regiment during their Middle East service, 1915–16, show that old brass shoulder titles 'SIY' (Shropshire Imperial Yeomanry) had been taken into use. These were worn together with a curved cloth pattern consisting of the white letters 'SHROPSHIRE YEO.' on a red background.

H4: Cloth shoulder title, 2/18th (County of London) Bn., The London Regiment (London Irish Rifles)

H5, H6: Medal ribbons for Territorial Decoration and Efficiency Medals

The combination of the Yeomanry (yellow) and

Scouts, 1/6th or 1/8th Bns., Royal Warwickshire Regiment in Italy, 1918. These battalions were identified by a wide vertical bar worn on the upper arm—red for 1/6th, blue for 1/8th. Companies were also indicated by coloured cloth facing the whole of the shoulder straps—blue for 'A', red for 'B', yellow for 'C' and green for 'D'. (Mike Chappell)

Volunteer (green) medal ribbons in 1908 produced the pattern shown in H5, the officers' Decoration ribbon being slightly wider than that of the men's Efficiency Medal. In the Honourable Artillery Company a special design based on the racing colours of Edward VII was worn for both awards (H6).

H7: Private, 1/5th Battalion, Royal Warwickshire Regiment; Italy, 1918

The four battalions of the Royal Warwickshire Regiment in 143rd Infantry Brigade, 48th (South Midland) Division wore red or blue battalion devices on sleeves and helmet covers. Patches were sewn to shoulder straps to indicate the wearer's company, blue being 'A' Company.

H8: In some units of 48th (South Midland) Division the Divisional sign—a white diamond—was painted on the helmets with the cap badge superimposed: (H8) is that of the Divisional Pioneers, the 1/5th (Cinque Ports) Battalion, Royal Sussex Regiment.

H9: Private, 1/7th Battalion, King's (Liverpool Regiment); France, 1918

Note the divisional sign of the 55th (West Lancashire) Division—the red rose; the battalion/brigade indicator worn on the back; and the company indicator on the shoulder strap.

H10: Armoured car, Westmorland and Cumberland Yeomanry, 1915

Two armoured cars are known to have been used by the Westmorland and Cumberland Yeomanry for home service during the war. Provided by a special fund, the vehicles were built by the Guy Lewin Company of London on Italian-made Issotta-Fraschini chassis. Note the long narrow rifle-slits with sliding covers, and spotlight on the roof.

Officers of 'A' Company, 1st Honourable Artillery Company at Montreuil, France, November 1918. Taken just after the signing of the Armistice, this photograph includes 2nd Lt. R. Hughesdon (standing left) who won both the Distinguished Conduct Medal and Military Medal while serving in the ranks. Seated front are three officers who gained the Military Cross—from left to right, Lt. R. J. Fowles, Lt. A. W. Hawes, and Capt. R. Spicer.

Notes sur les planches en couleur

Les lecteurs doivent vérifier ces notes en utilisant les légendes sur les peintures et les légendes en anglais dans le texte.

A1 Grande tenue, caractéristique des uniformes flamboyants de la 'Yeomanry' (un équivalent pourrait être la Garde à cheval, recrutée parmi les petits propriétaires terriens) dans les styles traditionnels de la cavalerie. Les sergents des régiments portaient un badge spécial sur le bras droit, au-dessus des chevrons jusqu'en 1900, sur les chevrons après cela; notez également le badge d'instructeur pour les signaux avec drapeaux entrecroisés. Les étoiles sur la manche indiquent chacune quatre années de service qualifié. A2 Uniforme complet de style Lancier, avec calot. Le badge de renard fait référence à l'origine de l'unité formée par des fermiers et propriétaires terriens venant d'un pays grand amateur de la chasse au renard. A3 Uniforme de grande tenue de style Dragon, complet avec ceinturon à munitions, orné, d'officier. A4 Coiffure d'officier de style lancier de la 'Yeomanry' du Lincolnshire. A5 Type unique de casque de cuir porté par la 'Yeomanry' du Norfolk. A6 Badge de coiffure de la 'Yeomanry' du Berkshire, rappelant l'ancien dessin de cheval gravé dans la craie des collines au-dessus d'Uffington.

B1 Levé parmi des Ecossais dans Liverpool et ses environs, ce bataillon portait des kilts en tartan de modèle Forbes, une tunique sans pareille en gris olivâtre avec des parements écarlates, et un équipement en cuir brun. La patte d'épaule est présentée dans le dessin de détail. B2 Levée auprès du personnel de services comme les Postes, le Trésor public, et l'Amirauté, cette unité a conservé son uniforme de Volontaires dont le style date des années 1860 en gris et bleu. B3 Seul l'insigne sur la patte d'épaule distingue cet uniforme de celui des bataillons dits 'Regular' du régiment dont ils relevaient. Le badge des trois 'Ss' dans un cercle à couronne identifiait la

Farbtafeln

A1 Galauniform, typisch für die extravaganten Husaren in den traditionellen Kavallerie-Stilarten. Die Unteroffiziere trugen ein spezialabzeichen am linken Aem über dem Winkel (bis 1900), später auf den Winkeln. Siehe auch die gekreuzten Flaggen eines Signal-Instruktors. Die Sterne am Ärmel zeigen jeweils vier qualifizierte Dienstjahre an. A2 Galauniform im Lancer-Stil, mit Käppi. Das Fuchs-Abzeichen weist auf den Ursprung der Einheit unter Farmern und Lanadel in Fuchsjagd-Gemeinschaften hin. A3 Dragonerartige Galauniform mit verziertem Offiziersgürtel mit Taschen. A4 Lancerartiger Offiziershelm aus Lincolnshire. A5 Einzigartige Form eines Lederhelms der Norfolk-Yeomanry. A6 Berkshire Yeomanry.Kappenabzeichen, erinnernd an die uralte Pferdefigur, die über Uffingdon in den Kalksteinhügel eingeschnitten wurde.

B1 Bestehend aus Schotten aus und um Liverpool, trug das Bataillon Kilts aus Forbes-Tartan, eine einzigartigegraubraune jacke mit scharlachroten Aufschlägen und braunes Lederriemenzeug. Der Schulterriemen wird in der detaillierten Zeichnung gezeigt. B2 Diese Einheit, bestehend aus früheren Angehörigen der Post, der Steuerbehörde und der Admiralität behielten ihre Freiwilligen-Uniformen im Stil der 60er Jahre des 19.Jahrhunderts in Grau und Blau. B3 Nur die Schulterriemenabzeichen unterscheiden diese Uniform von von der regulären Bataillone des Mutterregiments. Das Abzeichen mit den drei 'S' in einem gekrönten Kreis kennzeichnet die Special Service Section—freiwillige Einheiten, die kurzfristig für heimatsverteidigungszwecke einberufen werden konnten. In den Deatils sind die Schulterriemen-Abzeichen zu zehene. B4 Kappenabzeichen, Abbildung B1. B5 Kappenabzeichen, 5. Bn., Seaforth Highlanders. B6 Kappenabzeichen, Buckinghamshire Bn., Oxfordshire & Buckinghamshire Light Infantry.

Section de Service Spécial—des unités qui se portaient volontaires pour être appelées sur brève notification dans les urgences, pour des missions de défense intérieure. Le detail montre l'insigne de patte d'épaule. **B4** Détail de badge de la coiffure, figure **B1**. **B5** Badge de la coiffure, '5th Bn., Seaforth Highlanders'. **B6** Badge de coiffure, 'Buckinghamshire Bn., Oxfordshire & Buckinghamshire Light Infantry'.

C1 Il porte l'insigne de bataillon en bleu et noir; trois chevrons pour service à l'étranger en bleu; le badge des Transmissions (d'où son équipement pour pistolet plutôt que fusil); et deux raies dorées enroulées sur la manche gauche. Details: badge de coiffure et insigne de patte d'épaule. **C2** Notez la silhouette de dragon noir portée sous le col dans ce bataillon, qui subit de lourdes pertes à Ypres le 8 mai 1915. Quelques officiers utilisaient l'équipement en toile et les fusils de soldats. **C3** Uniforme tropical utilisé en Inde, avec insigne détachable. Détails: écusson de casque, et insigne fabriqué localement sur la patte d'épaule. **C4** Badge de l'Honourable Artillery Company'; et insigne de patte d'épaule, porté avec un 'A' ou un 'B' par les deux batteries d'artillerie. **C5** Badge des Cyclistes des Highlands, et une variation d'insigne de patte d'épaule.

D1 Notez le badge de 'bombe', et les sacs à munitions pour 10 grenades; des chiffres blancs sur found rouge identifiaient les unités de la 125th Brigade. Des unités de la Territoriale affiliées aux régiments de Fusiliers portaient la 'bombe' des Fusiliers sur les pattes d'épaule ainsi que d'autres insignes, leur longueur supplémentaire les faisant souvent casser, elles furent ainsi souvent éliminées pendant les combats. **D2** Les compagnies de mitrailleuse de la division avaient chacune leur propre écusson dans la 42nd Div.; notez le badge de mitrailleur blanc et kaki, le badge de 'range-finder' et le chevron de bonne conduite. **D3** Manoeuvrant un mortier Stokes équipé d'une suspente et de poignées pour le transport pendant l'avancée, il a le badge à bombe, bleu, d'un opérateur de mortier, une raie enroulée, le chevron de bonne conduite (pour deux années de service) et les lettres 'LM' —pour mortier léger—sur un fond de la couleur identifiant la 126th Brigade. **D4–12** Une sélections d'écussons de manche, etc., portés dans la 42nd Division: **D4** de gauche à droite: artillerie de la division 'RAHQ, 210th & 211th Brigades', colonne de munition et batteries de mortier de tranchée X et Y. **D5** 42nd Division, état-major du quartier général divisionnaire, 19e Section Vétérinaire Mobile, '239th Div. Employment Company', et 'pionier battalion'. **D6** Trois compagnies de combat, 'Royal Engineers'. **D7** '125th Bde.—1/5th, 1/7th, 1/8th Lancs. Fusiliers'. **D8** '126th Bde.—1/5th E. Lancs., 1/8th & 1/10th Manchesters'. **D9** '127th Bde.—1/5th, 1/6th, 1/7th Manchesters'. **D10** Mitrailleurs—Quartier général, Compagnies A à D respectivement. **D11** Trois unités d'ambulance de campagne 'RAMC'. **D12** Unités de l''Army Service Corps'.

E1 Les bicyclettes actuelles avaient disparu depuis longtemps; cette unité d'une pauvre qualité médicale était vêtue d'habits conçus par Shackleton, l'explorateur du Pôle, avec des armes russes. Notez le badge à étoile de la force expéditionnaire. **E2** L'un des deux bataillons portant le kilt des 'HLI', vêtu pour des travaux difficiles à Gallipoli; notez la 'flamme' du casque et l'insigne de patte d'épaule. **E3** Bataillon (une pelle rouge), compagnie (barre bleue) et insigne de tireur d'élite (une bande verte autour de la manchette). **E4** 'Flammes' de manche de la 161st Brigade, 54th Div.: '1/4th, 1/5th, 1/6th, 1/7th Essex Regt'. **E5** Insigne de patte d'épaule de style Fusiliers, '4th Bn. Royal Scots, 7th Bn. West Yorks. Regt'. **E6** Insigne de la 46th Division, portée au col: de haut en bas, '1/1st Bn. Monmouths, 1/5th N. Staffords, 1/4th Leicesters, 1/7th Sherwood Foresters'.

F1 Deux raies rouges de manchette indiquent le rang: le grand 'T' en argent au coin de la cape identifiait le service, de même que le badge (voir **F4**). Le bonnet de paille était une coiffure portée en dehors du service. **F2** Notez l'insigne de patte d'épaule du cycliste, le badge de bras; et le badge de Service Impérial à droite sur la poitrine, marquant les unités volontaires pour le service à l'étranger. **F3** Formé par des employés de la 'Royal Aircraft Factory, Farnborough'. **F4** Voir **F1**. **F5–F8** Voir légendes en anglais pour l'identification.

G1 Notez la flamme de casque régimentaire, la flamme sur la manche, et l'insigne de patte d'épaule. **G2, G3** Notez le titre en tissu sur la manche, et l'écusson rouge de bataillon dans la séquence adoptée par la 56th Division; les officiers portaient la croix noir au dos de la tunique et du casque. **G4** Flammes de bataillons, 'West. Yorks. Regt. Territorials—'T' pour 1/5th–1/8th Bns.', des cercles pour '2/5th–2/8th'. **G5** Flammes d'unité de la 61st Div.—carré, triangle et cercle pour les '182nd, 183rd, 184th Brigades'. Dans les deux premières brigades, la séquence de bataillon était rouge, bleu, jaune, noir, avec vert et pourpre/rose pour mitrailleurs et opérateurs de mortier de tranchée. La '184th Bde.' utilisait les couleurs jaune, rouge, noir, bleu clair pour les bataillons d'infanterie. Sont illustrés: '2/5th Royal Warwicks, 2/6th Glosters, 2/5th Glosters, 182nd MG Coy, 2/8th Worcesters'. **G6–G10** Voir légendes en anglais pour identification.

H1 Kilt et hauts de chaussettes en gris Hodden, pompon de coiffure bleu et languettes de chaussettes identifiaient les 'London Scottish'; le triangle rouge marque la '56th Div.' **H2–H4** Voir légendes en anglais. **H5**, **H6** Rubans de médailles, Décoration de la Territoriale et Médailles d'efficacité. **H7** Les flammes de bataillon étaient portées sur les manches et les couvre-casques, des flammes de compagnie sur les pattes d'épaule—ici A Coy. **H8** 'Pionier Bn., 48th Div.', un bataillon du Régiment du Sussex. **H9** Signe de la division, une rose rouge; flamme de la brigade et de la division portée au dos; flamme de la compagnie sur les pattes d'épaule. **H10** Voiture blindée fabriquée dans le privé pour mission de défense intérieure.

C1 Er trägt die Bataillons-Insignien in Blau und Schwarz; drei Überseedienst-Winkel in Blau; ein Signalmann-Abzeichen (deshalb die Pistole anstatt eines Gewehrs); und schließlich zwei Goldstreifen am linken Ärmel, die zwei Verwundungen anzeigen. **C2** Siehe schwarze Drachen-Silhouette, die unterhalb des Kragens in diesem Bataillon getragen wurde, das am 8.Mai 1915 schwere Verluste in Ypres erlitt. Manche Offiziere benutzten Soldatengurte und Gewehre. **C3** In indien getragene Tropenuniform mit abnehmbaren Insignien. Detail: Helmabzeichen und örtlich angefertigte Schulterriemenabzeichen. **C4** Abzeichen der Honourable Artillery Company; Schulterabzeichen Mit Aufschrift 'A' oder 'B' für die beiden Artillerie-Batterien. **C5** Abzeichen der Highland Cyclists, und eine Variation der Schulterabzeichen.

D1 Siehe 'Bomben'-Abzeichen und Taschen für 10 Granaten; weiße Zahlen auf rotem Grund identifizieren Einheiten der 125. Brigade. Territorial-Einheiten die an die Füsilier-Regimenter angeschlossen waren, trugen die Füsilier-'Bombe' zusammen mit anderen Abzeichen auf den Schulterriemen, die aufgrund ihrer zusätzlichen Länge oft rissen, so daß sie im Feld häufig nicht getragen wurden. **D2** Jede der MG-Kompanien der Division hatte in der 42. Division eigene Abzeichen; siehe weiß-khakifarbenes Abzeichen der MG-Schützen, 'Zielsucher-Abzeichen' und Winkel für gut verrichteten Dienst. **D3** Er bedient einen Stokes-Granatwerfer, mit einer Schlinge und Traggriffen für den Vormarsch, und er trägt das blaue Bomben Abzeichen des Granatwerferschützen, einen Streifen für eine Verwundung, den Winkel für zwei Jahre gut verrichteten Dienst und die Buchstaben 'LM' (Light mortar = leichter Granatwerfer) auf dem Untergrind der Farbe der 126. Brigade. **D4–12**: Eine Auswahl von Ärmelabzeichen usw., die in der 42. Division getragen wurden: **D4** von links nach rechts: Divisions-artillerie—RAHQ, 210. & 211. Brigade, Munitionseinheit, und Schützengraben-Granatwerferbatterien X und Y. **D5** 42. Division, Stab des Divisionshauptquartiers 19. Mobile Veterinary Section, 239. Div. Employment Company und Pionier-Bataillon. **D6** Drei Feldkompanien, Royal Engineers. **D7** 125. Bde.—1/5., 1/7., 1/8. Lancashire Fusiliers. **D8** 126. Bde.—1/5. E. Lancs., 1/8. & 1/10. Manchesters. **D9** 127. Bde.—1/5., 1/6., 1/7. Manchesters. **D10** MG-Schützen—HQ, jeweils A-D-Kompanien. **D11** Drei RAMC-Feldabulanz-Einheiten. **D12** Einheiten des Army Service Corps.

E1 Die Fahrräder waren schon seit langem verschwunden; diese Einheit geringer medizinischer Qualität trug Kleidung, die vom Polarforscher Shackleton entworfen war, und russische Waffen. Siehe Star-Abzeichen der Expeditionary Forces. **E2** Eines von zwei in Kilts gekleideten Bataillonen des HLI, ausgerüstet für schweren Einsatz bei Gallipoli; siehe Helmabzeichen und Schulterriemen-Insignien. **E3** Abzeichen f. Bataillon (roter Spaten), Kompanie (blauer Streifen) und Scharfschützen (grünes Band um Manschette). **E4** Ärmelabzeichen f. 161. Bde., 54. Div.: 1/4., 1/5., 1/6., 1/7. Essex Regiment. **E5** Schulterriemen-Abzeichen der Rifles, 4. Bn., Royal Scots, 7. Bn., West Yorkshire Regiment. **E6** Abzeichen der 46. Div., unter dem Kragen getragen: von oben nach unten: 1/1. Bn. Monouths, 1/5. N. Staffords, 1/4. Leicesters, 1/7. Sherwood Foresters.

F1 Zwei rote Manschettenstreifen als Rangabzeichen; großes silbernes 'T' auf dem Umhang kennzeichnete die Waffengattung, ebenso wie ein Abzeichen (siehe **F4**). Der Stohhut wurde außer Dienst getragen. **F2** Siehe Radfahrers Schulterriemen-Abzeichen, Ärmelabzeichen; Imperial Service-abzeichen rechts auf der Brust als Kennzeichen für Freiwilligen-Einheit für den Dienst in Übersee. **F3** Zusammengestellt aus Personal der Royal Aircraft-Fabrik, Farnborough. **F4** siehe **F1**. **F5–F8** Für Identifizierung siehe englischsprachige Bildtexte.

G1 Siehe Regiments-Helmabzeichen, Ärmelabzeichen und Schulterriemen-Insignien. **G2** Siehe Stoff-'Titles' am Ärmel und rote Bataillons-Abzeichen, in der Sequenz der 56. Div.; Offiziere trugen das schwarze Kreuz auf der Rückseite von Blusen und Helmen. **G4** Bataillons-Abzeichen, West Yorks. Regt. Territorials—'T' für Bataillone 1%.—1/8., Kreise für 2/5.—2/8. **G5** 61. Division, Division—Vierecke, Dreiecke und Kreise für 182., 183. und 184. Brigade. Bei den beiden ersten Brigaden war die Sequenz rot, blau, gelb, schwarz; mit grün und violett/rosa für MG-Schützen und Granatwerfer-Schützen. Die 184. Brigade hatte gelb, rot, schwarz, hellblau für Infanteriebataillone. Abgebildet: 2/5. Royal Warwicks, 2/6. Glosters, 2/5. Glosters, 182. MG-Komp., 2/8. Worcesters. **G6–G10** Siehe englischsprachige Bildtexte zur Identifikation.

H1 Kilt in 'Hodden grey' wie Sockenoberteile, blaues Pompon an kappe und Sockenabzeichen identifizierten das London Scottish, das rote Dreieck, die 56. Div. **H2–H4** Siehe englischsprachige Bildtexte. **H5**, **H6** Ordensspangen, Territorial-Auszeichnung, Leistungsmedaillen. **H7** Bataillonsabzeichen an Ärmeln und Helmbedeckungen, Kompanieabzeichen an Schulterriemen—hier Kompanie A. **H8** Pionier Bn., 48. Div., ein Bataillon im Sussex-Regiment. **H9** Rote Rose, Divisionsabzeichen; Brigaden- und Bataillonsabzeichen am Rücken; Kompanieabzeichen auf Schulterriemen. **H10** Gepanzertes Fahrzeug, privat hergestellt für Einsatz bei Inlandverteidigung.